Buried Deep in Shallow Ground

Leaving Childhood Behind

Honor Harlow

Copyright © 2022 Honor Harlow

978-1-914225-92-5

All intellectual property rights including copyright, design right and publishing rights rest with the author. No part of this book may be copied, reproduced, stored or transmitted in any way including any written, electronic, recording, or photocopying without written permission of the author. This is a work of fiction. All the main character in this publication are fictitious and any resemblance to a real person is purely coincidental. Published in Ireland by Orla Kelly Publishing. Edited by Red Pen Edits.

I wish to dedicate this book to all the people who had to leave their homes in Ireland. It is especially dedicated to all the girls and women who packed the little they had, boarded a train that took them to a boat that carried them away from all that was familiar. They departed, not knowing what awaited them in the strange land they were going to.

I admire and salute these women for their strength and resilience.

I wish to acknowledge all the help my daughter has given me. Without her, this book would never have been written.

Contents

Prologue	ix
Secondary School	1
We Were Changing	16
1967	24
Jackie Kennedy's Visit to Dublin	28
Second Year 1967-68	33
The Paper Round	40
The Cinema	43
Mass On Sunday	51
Study Time	62
The Wake	65
1968	72
The Youth Club	88
Getting the Hall Ready	95
We Meet At Mass	104
Friday 13th	122
Summer Ends	136
1969-1972	141
September 1969	156
Fifth Year	163
First Love	175
The Bones in the Home	183
The Art Studio	195

Contents Cont.

Driving Lessons	200
Evelyn and Ricky	211
People in Wheelchairs	225
My Own Car	237
News for Kait	242
The Blonde Blake	250
The Next Day	255
Letters	266
Please Review	271
About the Author	272

Town Map of Drumbron

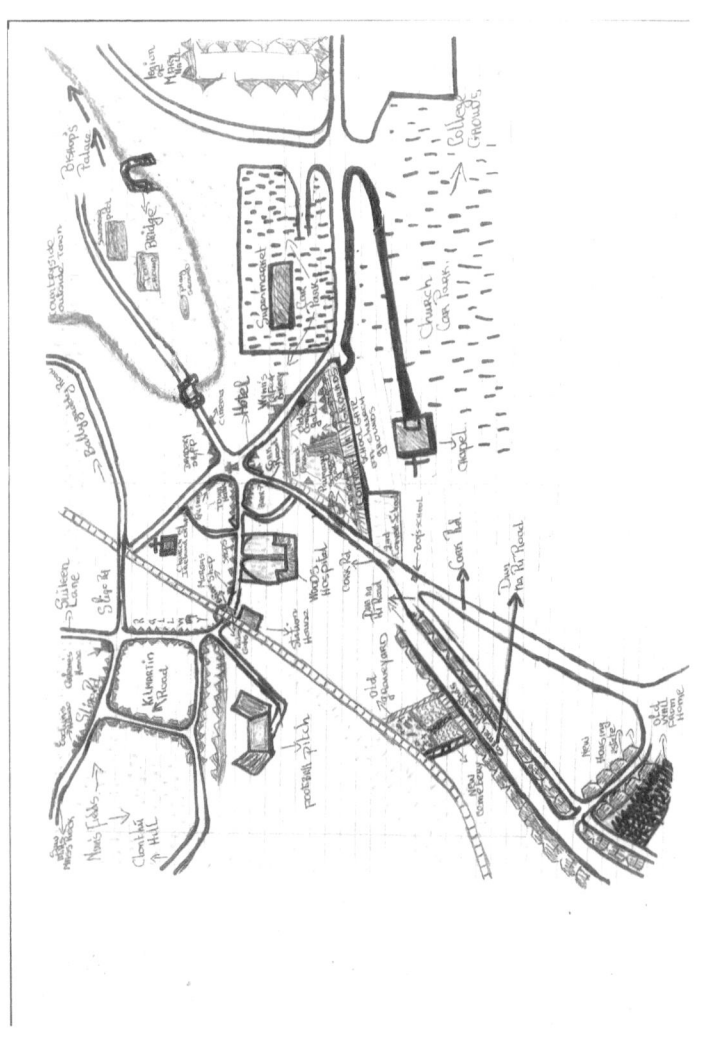

Prologue

Everyone in Drumbron thought the Mother & Baby Home closed because Hurricane Debbie blew the slates off the roof, but I knew that was not true. Nan Gormley and Nanny Ward told my friends and me the real reason.

"The inspector took it into his head to pay a surprise visit and that is what got it shut down," Nan said.

"And don´t forget the other two men he dragged along with him, Mary," Nanny reminded her.

This made me say, "The inspector was big like Cú Chulainn if he was able to drag two men along with him."

"*A grá mo croí*, it's a way of saying he got them to go there against their will. What Moll is saying is that he fooled them into going to the Home unbeknownst to the nuns."

"What did it matter if the nuns knew the men were coming or not?" I wanted to know.

"They didn't have time to hide away them children that weren't right, like the other times.

"What other times?"

"The visits when they were told the inspectors were coming and the nuns hid the sick cráturs out of the way."

"Sick cráturs?"

"The cratureens that weren't normal, even though they came into the world as right as rain."

I didn't know those children, only the ones who came to our class. I asked Nan and Nanny where our Home Babies would live if the Home was closed. They told me not to worry as the children from Drumbron would be sent to other Homes around the country.

I didn't like that because it meant I wouldn't be able to see Brigid or Liam if they went to a different Home. I had *grá* on the two of them.

Brigid was tall and a bit like me, only her hair was blonde and not black like mine but the dimple on her chin was the same as my one and my daddy's.

Liam was skinny and miserable-looking and wore a *geansaí* knitted with lines of different coloured wool. It had snots on the cuffs of the sleeves, but I didn't care.

I wanted Liam as my brother because my own brother was in Limbo. My daddy buried him in a shoebox one night near the Mass Rock. Úna told me that was where they put the babies with no names.

Úna is one my three best friends. The other two are Kait and Evelyn. I am glad they are my pals, and that we are starting secondary school together.

Secondary School

On the first day of secondary school, I waited for Úna, Kait and Evelyn outside the gate on Church Street. Looking at the dark and gloomy grey wall surrounding the narrow, metal doorway I shivered and wished I was outside the bright, lacy railings and wide gates that were the entrance to the primary school or even at the gate of the nun's residence near Chapel Lane, which was normal and not scary thanks to Joe Daly. After the Vatican Council, he knocked down the nun's high wall and put in a normal gate and railings. I liked trailing my hand along the twisty bits stuck between the bars of the railings, imagining they were metal cobwebs.

We could easily have used that bright entrance but because the nun's bedroom windows overlooked the tarmac driveway, we were told to use the gate on Church Street instead. It seems the auld nuns complained that noisy girls were galloping past their windows, not letting them say their prayers in peace. So, because of that, I was in front of this grim, grey wall with the life frightened out of me.

I stared at the gate, hidden deep inside the menacing bulging wall of craggy-bellied stones plastered with cement, darken by years, and shuddered. The breath of the wall was so wide that it needed two lines of spiked glass on top, vigilant and ready to rip flesh, if anyone was stupid enough to try to climb over it. It looked like a fortress, a prison you went into and never came out of, like the nuns who spent their lives there. Even when they died, they were buried in their own graveyard, with no one from town going to their funerals.

I stood quivering, convincing myself my friends would never show. Only when I saw Kait and Ev coming out of Wynn's shop across the road wearing the school uniform did the fearfulness leave me. I waved at them and then Úna appeared, walking real fast, as though trying to leave her uniform behind her. We hugged, delighted to see each other. Then Evelyn stood back and took charge shooting orders at us.

"Get in quick before any of the boys come along and start mocking us when they see in these clothes."

I hesitated, still in two minds about going in, but the sugary bun Evelyn had bought in Wynn's and eaten crossing the street, propelled her into action. She pushed open the heavy gate that shrieked on its hinges, letting us know it was not welcoming in the light from the street or us. She shoved me through the narrow gap. Against my will, I was on the other side of the wall that wore a crown of prickly glass. The others tiptoed in behind me shielded by my height. Once we knew there were no monsters lurking behind the door, our bodies lost the tenseness and Ev was able to say what was really worrying her.

"When the boys see us in this uniform, they are going to slag us no end."

"How are they going to see us, Ev?" Kait asked, sweeping her eyes around the cement ground where not even a weed dared to grow.

"The College is just up the road and the lads from the Brothers come down to Wynn's at midday as well," she who knew these things informed us, looking both ways to see if any of the boys had gotten into the fortified enclosure of purity and chastity.

"Who cares about what the boys say? Let them mock us if they want," I replied but it didn't help Ev.

Tugging at the beige blouse that was part of the school uniform, she said, "God, to think I'll have to wear this shitty colour for the next five years is giving me the willies."

"At least the pinafore is brown," Kait said trying to console Ev.

"Ya! A darker shade of shite, like when you are constipated, so shut up, Kait. Let's see what this place is like," Ev commanded and led us further in. We followed her to the small cobblestone courtyard where we saw a small crowd of girls standing looking lost and frightened.

We edged our way towards the forlorn girls, slithering silently so as not to draw the attention of the bigger ones, who were strutting around the yard or flying over to a girl, yapping non-stop as they wrapped their arms around them. We gazed open-mouthed and dumbstruck at these seemingly grown-up girls talking loudly and laughing with no nun around to put a halt to their fun. Just as we were becoming used to the strangeness of it, the bigger girls started drifting towards the wooden door lodged in the square structure standing to the side of the courtyard. As they disappeared through the weighty door of a hundred cracks, so too did the rigidness holding us stiff. Our necks could once again move in different directions allowing us to gawk at the craggy two-storey, flat-roofed building the big girls had vanished into. The long, narrow glass panes of the white windows that were only missing iron grids to make it a jail window, left us intrigued.

As though to answer our curiosity about what was in this place, a nun appeared at the entrance, beckoning us to follow her. We trailed behind her up wide, wooden, dipping steps of stairs to a small landing. She crossed it, opened the first door of the two facing us. We followed her into a big hall with long, old-fashioned, sash windows of many squares at each end of it. The hall was full of desks, half of them turned towards one of the windows and the other lot looked at the window on the opposite wall of the long room.

The nun walked towards one window, stood on a podium and made a coughing sound. When all heads were looking at her, she explained there were two classes A and B. From the list in her hands, she called out the names of the girls who were in the A class and told them to stand in a group. Most were boarders, while the day girls, who were the town and country girls, were on the B class list.

After the name-calling, the nun showed two boarders how to pull a panel that went from the floor to the ceiling across the middle of the hall. It became two classrooms with windows and doors of their own. We sat down.

Our first day at secondary school had begun.

The class-dividing nun told us to where to sit and left. We sat still, ears listening to the sound of legs pushing against cloth coming up the stairs, our eyes stayed glued to the door until the owner of the skirt, a small, thin nun, stood on the threshold. She walked in and stood in front of the blackboard and disappeared except for her pink face, white bib and the band on her head. We stood up as we were used to doing all our lives.

She told us to sit down and explained in Irish that she was the Irish teacher, and her name was Sister Agatha. She called the roll and before we knew it, she was leaving. Evelyn made the most of this time we were on our own whispering she hoped 'Miss Marple' wouldn't be a good detective and find out what we were up to. All of us were fans of Agatha Christie, so we were laughing when the next nun came in.

Leaving Childhood Behind

It was a Sister Beatriz, who was our Botany and Art teacher. She asked our names and little else before the bell rang. As the nun left, Evelyn christened her Beetroot behind her hand to us. We heard the desks in other classrooms being rattled and girls shuffling down the stairs, so we did likewise as we supposed it was playtime. We moved slowly down the stairs one after the other, like we had done in primary school, thinking any minute now a nun will order us to make a line, but no one was watching over us.

In the yard, we were left to our own devices. We were trusted not to fight or pull each other's hair. Stupefied, wandering around, we bumped into some older town-girls we knew.

We asked why we didn't make a line to go out for playtime in awed voices. They laughed, saying it was 'the break' and not playtime. Then we told them about the nuns coming in and out of the classroom and about the two brand-new nuns we had never seen before. They explained we'd have a teacher for every subject. Then they told us the girls in Class A were doing Latin instead of Art, as they came from posh families, and if they wanted to become doctors or lawyers, they needed Latin.

Break finished. We climbed the stairs slowly while the older girls ran, shouted and pushed each other. We looked at them with wide eyes, surprised at how daring they were.

Back in class, our eyes became even bigger and nearly shot out of our heads when the next teacher came into the room. She was a woman, wearing a grey suit and a dark blouse and had shoes with a little heel. She introduced herself as Miss Prior and told us she was the English teacher. Later on, we had another lay teacher, Miss Grey, who wore make-up and taught History and Geography. During the day, we got to know the rest of the teachers, like Sister Peter, the Domestic teacher. Evelyn didn't give her a nickname. However, Sister Dorothy, the Maths teacher, became Dots.

During the first days, we stood awkward and perplexed in this new and strange world. We town-girls had the advantage over the boarders and country-girls in at least knowing lots of the girls, as we had been at school together in Drumbron since Low Babies. For most of the other girls, the beginning of first year was like Christopher Columbus' journey to the Indies in that all was new.

We discovered exotic girls from far-away places such as Corofin or Dundearg miles outside Drumbron. They cycled in and out to school every day, even if it was raining. There was a small, foxy haired country girl called Catherine who lived near the Sandy Hills. She sat behind Úna and me. Fionnuala, or Nuala as she wanted to be called, the Drumbron girl who was good at drawing, sat beside her. Their desk was in front of Kait and Evelyn, so they were in between us like the butter on a sandwich.

As the months went on, Nuala and Catherine sort of became half members of our gang. When me or Úna wanted to say something to Kait or Evelyn, we got them to pass on the message. Catherine was shy and not bold like us. Nuala lived in the same kind of house as Kait's and Úna, so they considered her a neighbour because the street where she lived, Tobair Benin Road, was around the corner from Dun na Rí, Úna's street.

There were boarders in our class from other counties miles away. We looked at them as though they were from another planet because I was the only one out of our gang who had gone outside County Galway to Sligo and Cavan.

Leaving Childhood Behind

When we talked to the country girls and the boarders, we town girls realised we were the luckiest ones of all. We had our dinner at home with our mammies while the country girls ate sandwiches and had nothing hot until they cycled out to their houses. The boarders didn't even see their mammies, daddies, brothers and sisters in the evening. They had to wait until the holidays.

The newness of everything kept us in our place at first. However, as the months went by, we became bolder. As soon as one teacher left the classroom to go to another room, we talked instead of brushing up on the lesson for the next class, as we had done at first.

The breaks between classes became chatty affairs but never enough time to say what we wanted. So, instead of sitting cowed or in awe of the teacher, we talked behind our hands or dropped something on the floor so we could turn around and talk to the girl behind.

There was so much to talk about, like the films we had seen or trashing out the merits of *Lovely Leitrim* versus the Beatles' *Day Tripper*. Frank Sinatra's songs, like *Strangers in the Night*, were never talked about because the old people liked him, so he couldn't be hip. Even the most important news had to be doled out because time was scarce, so the time Úna was dying, it took her the whole morning to tell us. Getting the details of her sickness was more nerve-racking than the Saturday matinee film sequels we saw in the Odeon, where every week, the good guy was in terrible danger. We'd have to wait until the following Saturday to see if the train would run over his body tied on the tracks or if he would manage not to fall to his death below as he clung onto the cliff edge by his fingertips. Úna did her best to tell us all the story of her dying, and it wasn't her fault we heard it in snatches. She started telling us the first part on *An Lár*, where we met every morning to walk to school together. When she saw me and Kait waiting, she rushed over, saying she had something very important to tell us, but she couldn't start until Evelyn arrived, which she did after what seemed like ages. We gathered close around Úna as we walked, and she told us how she was dying.

"Yesterday evening about the time the Angelus was ringing, I felt a tickling between my legs." Us three looked at her wondering what that had to do with dying.

"Why didn't you check to see what it was?" Ev asked as we thought there was no big deal about being itchy.

"I was at study, like ye were, so I couldn't. Janey Macs, the itch was driving me crazy."

"Maybe you wet yourself?" Kait said and we stopped and smiled at Úna to let her know that even if she had, we were still her friends.

"I was thinking that too and that the wee was trickling down, causing the wet feeling between my legs."

"It would be terrible if you did wet yourself."

"I know, so that is why I said to Sr Beatriz, '*An bhfuil cead agam dul amach?*'"

"That was the best thing to do." By now we had reached the classroom and she continued telling us in a low voice.

"Well, as soon as I got inside the toilet, I bolted the door so no one could walk in on me. Then I touched my gigeen," Úna said.

"You didn't!" Evelyn roared in shock, without realising she was shouting. Sister Agatha was down at our desk.

"*An bhfuil siad ag caint?*"

"*Nílimid*," we all said at the same time, but the nun stayed standing by our desk and because of that, it wasn't until the break that we heard the full story.

On the way down the stairs Evelyn said, "I betchya there was an earwig stuck in her knickers and that was what was causing the itch."

Sometimes when our mammies took in the washing from the line, there would be an earwig among the clothes, but Kait had a different idea.

"Twasn't. It was a hair, so it was," she said blushing. Me and Evelyn looked at her wondering why she had gone so red.

"What would a rib of hair be doing down there?" I asked in a mocking tone, not believing Kait could be such a silly goose thinking a rib of hair could fall into your knickers.

Kait got even redder and said in a low voice, "Cos they grow around your gigeen too."

"They don't," I said but Úna who was walking slowly behind us nodded her head, agreeing with Kait.

"You're codding! Hair only grows on your head, you silly goose."

Úna told me to shut up because what had happened to her was important and we had to know about it. Sitting on her haunches and us huddling around her in a corner of the yard, she whispered the rest of the story wanting only us to know and no one else, not even Nuala McCabe who had started to sort of hang around with us.

"When I took my hand away, the tips of my fingers were red with blood. I washed them but I was shaking with fright thinking all the blood in my body was spilling out through my gigeen."

"You poor thing," Kait said. "What did you do?"

"I went back to the study hall. Sr Beatriz was sitting on the high podium in the middle where she watches us study."

"Did ya tell her?"

"I didn't, just said I didn't feel well and was going home."

"But you were bleeding."

"I know I was, but my heart was in my mouth thinking I was going to die. I wanted to see Mammy before I died, so that's why I left and didn't tell the nun."

"You were right. Did your mother send for the doctor?" Ev asked.

"She didn't. She gave me a clatter across the head and told me to keep quiet in front of the small ones when I started screaming, 'Mammy, Mammy, I'm going to die! There's blood coming out of me!'"

"A clatter?" we all asked at once, this piece of the story being more surprising than what happens at the Matinee.

Úna shushed us by saying, "Yeah, a clatter." Then she continued. "She told me…"

"Why did she give you a clatter?" Ev insisted. She was still puzzled as to why any mother would hit you if you were dying.

"Because for some reason or other she was really cross and said to me, 'Get into that room there and wait until I am finished washing the spuds and have them on to boil, then I'll deal with you.'"

Being told to go into the room made Úna go out of her mind with worry because when any of the family were sick enough for the doctor to come, they were put into the downstairs bedroom to wait for him. She was in the sick room, but at the same time, she thought she couldn't be very bad if her mother had given her a wallop. Úna waited, biting her nails until the door was pushed open, and her mother told Úna what was wrong with her.

"What did she say?" Kait asked and we all gathered closed to Úna to hear if our friend was dying.

"That I was a woman."

"A woman? You're a girl," Ev said disappointed with that piece of news.

"She said I was a woman now and I had to be careful not to go too near a man."

"Not to stain him with the blood, is it?" I asked, thinking it had to be that but wanting to be sure.

"I don't know but she said the blood was normal and all women get it."

"I don't want to be a woman," I wailed.

"When you grow more, you'll be one too, whether you like it or not."

"I won't!" I insisted.

"Shut up, Arlene. Let Úna finish or we'll all be dead before we hear the rest of what happened."

"Mam gave me a piece of a thick towel and told me to put into my knickers. She said when she had money, she would buy a belt thing to hold the towel thing up."

"A belt?" I said thinking of the belts Daddy wears around his trousers and the ones Mammy has for her dresses which had buckles.

Kait asked, "A big towel?

"No, small like a face towel but it had loops at each end."

"Will you have blood every day?"

"No, Mam said it would stop after a few days but come back every now and then."

"Are you wearing the towel now?"

"Ya, that's why I'm walking slow, so it won't fall off."

"Is it full of blood."

"No, there only a spot or two. Mam gave me an auld towel that's no use and showed me how to make pads from it."

"Pads?" We all echoed in a surprised tone.

"Ya, to fit between my legs."

"Did you make any?"

"I made three last night because Mammy said I have to change them every day and soak them in cold water, so they are easier to wash."

"Wash the blood out, you mean?"

"Ya and I have to put the basin in the coal house."

"Why in the coal house?"

"So the young ones won't see them and ask questions."

For the next few weeks we spent every free minute wondering why girls bled and became women. Bleeding and sanitary towels was the theme of our conversations when we'd meet in *An Lár*, at break, as well as before and after study periods.

Did old women bleed too?

Did boys and men know girls bled?

If you didn't stop bleeding, would you die?

We wondered about all of these questions and also wondered if nuns, who spoke like women but didn't have hair, had periods?

Talking so much about blood coming out of the gigeen made us remember what Kait had said about hair growing on her gigeen. We wondered if she had told us the truth or was it just a story. Me and Ev asked her if it was really true hair grew on her gigeen.

"It does, so it does," she said and got red.

"I don't believe you. Come on, show us."

Kait got redder than the heart on the Sacred Heart. Her face bursting into flames was normal for us, so we kept on asking, even though she was nearly on fire.

"Oh shut up you two! Janey Macs, yer worse than Baby Patrick. Here, I'll show you mine," Úna said. It was ginger like the hair on her head. It stunned us into silence, although later we wondered if you had to comb it every morning for school.

Then at the beginning of second year, as though to teach me a lesson for not believing Kait, black hair started to grow under my armpits and around my gigeen.

The other two got their periods shortly after Úna's. Mine didn't come until a few months later. I wasn't frightened like Úna had been but at the same time I didn't tell Mammy I knew about periods because she would give me a lecture about 'nice girls not talking about certain things.' So I said, "Mammy, I'm bleeding. Will we go to Dr Kelly to see if I'm sick?"

"No, Mary. What is happening to you is that you are becoming a woman."

"A woman?"

"Yes, and it is important you say three Hail Marys night and morning for holy purity."

"Will holy purity stop the bleeding?"

"Mary! Don't be impertinent. Nice girls must be pure, so if you say your prayers, Our Lady will keep you safe."

"Alright, Mammy," was all I said, but I saw she was better than Úna's mammy because she bought sanity towels in the chemist for me. They were twelve pads of cotton wool inside gauzy material in a plastic bag. Mammy told me if I ever had to buy them myself, I had to wait until there was no man about to ask for them. She also said to wrap them in newspaper when I took them off. It was important they were hidden at the bottom of the rubbish bin, so no one would see them.

"Mammy, if everyone gets periods why do we have to be ashamed of them?"

"Mary, it's vulgar to talk about certain things. Modesty is a virtue and I want you to behave like a nice girl. Do you hear me?"

"A course I do," I said and walked out the door before she could say more.

The Terrible Twos

I was sick of listening to her and the other mothers complaining about us because we were teenagers. They said it was the terrible twos over again, only this time they couldn't pick up the cheeky, pimply smart-alec and carry us home. I told the girls what the coffee morning women had been saying about us.

"Pimply? No way!" Evelyn uttered in mock amazement.

We fell on the floor giggling because the pimple bit was true. Our flawless skin was plagued every so often by a pimple that left us in despair. The pimples would never appear in an out-of-the way place but smash bang on our nose, chin or forehead. We'd look in the mirror a hundred times to see if the ugly spot had shrunken and moan to each other how we were ashamed to leave the house with the enormous lump disfiguring our face.

Despite the pimples and not having white sets of perfect teeth like the Americans, who came with their parents to see the place where their grandparents had been born, we grew up in a time that was a great time to be a teenager in Ireland even though Mammy and Mr Delaney said the country was going to the dogs and that the young people should be reined in. They raged about pop music on the radio and having to listen to the Irish showbands really annoyed Mr Delaney.

"As if it isn't bad enough having a dance in the parish hall, now we hear them awful songs on the radio every day of our lives."

"I said to William things are getting out of hand. The priest letting them bring in an accordion or banjo player for social dances every now and again was fine, but now there's a dance there every Thursday night."

Mammy gave Daddy the blunt of her tongue for helping Fr Mannion and Miss Walsh in the dance hall that was on Barrack Street, a bit up from the Woods hospital. Still, it didn't surprise me because she liked nothing and especially not me going to the Odeon on Saturday nights to watch Sandra Dee and Troy Donohue or Doris Day and Rock Hudson. When I was small, I would have tried to please Mammy and not make her sick. Now I was beginning to think she was stupid. My pals thought the same about their parents too. Now that we were big, we knew better about things.

We Were Changing

Reading Bunty or Judy comics used to be wonderful. We waited every week to buy them and see what was happening to our friends 'The Four Marys.' The other girls on the pages of Bunty and Judy who went horse-riding looked so happy and we longed to go too, as well as do ballet like the girls with their tulle skirts and hair pulled back tight. Our lives revolved the next issue, wondering what would happen to such-and-such a girl. Now we thought them childish and predictable, even the new one called Mandy that had come out. We'd rather spend our money on magazines that had pictures and stories about The Monkees and Sandie Shaw. Sandie, with her hair swinging and her toes showing, was always on Top of the Pops.

Jimmy Saville was the best and we loved listening to him on the radio. We kept our fingers crossed we'd meet him in person one day. We imagined the fun we would have when we were with him and how the other girls would be jealous of us talking to him and getting his autograph. We listened to Terry Wogan on the radio but as he looked and sounded like all the men around about, we didn't care if we never met him.

The matinees with the good guy hanging off a cliff weren't as breath-taking as waiting to see if Sandra Dee would kiss Troy Donahue. The Tom and Gerry cartoons were so stupid, not half as funny as the Carry-On films. Lesley Philips only had to move a muscle in his face, and we were doubled over, falling off our seats with laughter.

The river got to be a dirty, messy and boring place to spend time. Sitting on the riverbank making daisy chains was alright for Úna's little brothers and sisters but now we thought it was childish and boring. We found it hard to think that we used to do such a horrible, disgusting thing as putting worms on a hook. Getting a lift from Kait's uncle and going to Salthill was better fun. Walking up and down the strand, sharing a candyfloss we had bought in one of the little colourful stands near the beach, was smashing. We'd tell the boys sitting on the wall we wouldn't give them any of our candyfloss, which usually made them come after us begging for a bite and talking to us.

Mammy loved watching television and tried to make me stay at home to watch The Late Show so I could learn to speak like Gay Byrne. She and Mr Delaney said Gay had a lovely accent and a very nice way of saying things. My mother was beginning to imitate how he spoke. It annoyed her when I didn't pronounce my words like Gay did.

At least I was not the only one who could not stand Gay Byrne. Mr McNulty, Úna's father, said Gay Byrne was a prissy mouth. I agreed and knew there was no way I would talk like him, in spite of Mammy insisting that I did. Then out of the blue, Mammy and Mr Delaney got upset with prissy-mouth.

"What happened, Mammy? Why are you so annoyed with Gay Byrne?"

"It's not Gay I am annoyed with. It's the woman giving the answer who is scandalous."

"What did she say?"

"What no decent woman should say."

Mr Delaney looked disgusted, saying no man had a right to ask a woman a question like that, even if he was Gay Byrne.

"But what did he ask?"

"Mary!" Mammy said crossly. "The less you know about this sort of thing the better."

"I want to know what they both said," I demanded, stamping my foot like when I was small.

"That's enough out of you. Get up those stairs to bed."

I went to my room but on Sunday I found out what they were angry about because Mr Delaney arrived at our house waving a newspaper. "Look, Dervla, the bishop agrees with us."

"About what, John?" Daddy, who was having breakfast at the table, enquired.

"About Gay asking that woman what she was wearing on her wedding night."

"John, please," Mammy said turning her eyes in my direction, "we mustn't talk about certain things."

"Dervla is right, John. Take it easy and let's have our breakfast in peace," Dad said, stabbing the sausage with his fork.

"Dervla has to know the bishop is as scandalised as we are."

"John, I'm having my rashers and eggs, and I don't want any bishop with them," objected Dad in his Garda's voice.

Mammy got up and went outside with Mr Delaney. I laughed and I was sorry Mrs McLoughlin didn't come on Sunday because she'd have shaken the mop at Mr Delaney and told him it was the nearest to Holy Water she could find.

The next day I was in the kitchen and heard Mammy telling Daddy about the bishop's outrage at a nightdress a woman didn't wear. Daddy nodded his head but didn't take his eyes from the newspaper.

Úna told us her father, Mr McNulty, was livid with the bishop. "A nice one to be talking, with him and all the other bishops going around wearing dresses."

Mr Kenny, Kait's father, was funny and made me and Ev laugh when he said, "McQuaid, the bollocks, is behind all this."

Kait's father used expressions that would have shocked Mammy, but they tickled me inside and made me want to laugh. Ev picked them up and was delighted to use them but when saying Mr Delaney was a right bollocks, she changed it to *boilg*, the Irish for stomach.

Me and Ev spent half the time in the Kenny house because the two of us lived nearby. Evelyn lived on Sligo Road, the street around the corner from Kilmartin Road, and it was no bother for her to pop up to Kait's house whenever she felt like it. For Úna it was more difficult as she lived a good bit away. When she was minding her baby brother, she wheeled the big pram through the town to be with us. Other days we took the shortcut up the tracks to her road, so the four of us were always together playing. For me, it was great not being in my house listening to Mammy and Mr Delaney talking and praising the town councillor who said, "The Late Late Show was a dirty programme that should be abolished altogether."

Blackboard Art

A few months after we started in First Year, two older girls came into our classroom and told us it was Sr Agatha's feast day and we had to decorate the blackboard.

"Who is the best at art?" they asked.

"Mary Blake and Nuala McCabe," everyone shouted back.

"Come here," they said. We got up slowly and walked towards the board where they were standing. "Write Happy Feast Day and use your imagination to decorate the board as though it was a birthday card," they said handing us a box of coloured chalk and then walked out the door.

Not having a clue what to do, I was looking at Nuala and she was looking at me when Ev piped up, "Happy Feast Day, my foot. It has to be in Irish so it will be *Lá Fhéile* something or other."

Ev and her idea were all we needed. Nuala started writing *Lá Breithe Shona* using the letters of the old Irish script, making it look like a page from the Book of Kells. As we worked, we seemed to read each other minds and knew exactly what we were doing. When we stood back, we found it hard to believe we had created such a wonderful work of art.

The whole board look like a book opened in the centre. The two middle pages, with the writing, were resting on the top of the other pages of the book, sloping down like the thinnest of steps until the borders of the brown cover showed.

The letter at the beginning of each sentence was curved and twisted like an animal or a snake, similar to how the monks in the monasteries had decorated the medieval manuscripts.

When Sr Agatha walked into room, we saw by the look on her face that she was amazed. It stayed on the board all day. As the other teachers wouldn't write on the board, it meant we didn't have to copy anything into our copybooks and had nearly a free day with no lessons.

Then the bell sounded for break, and we left the classroom. When we came back, the Reverend Mother and other nuns from the residence were admiring our artwork. Sr Agatha had left a bag of sweets on our desk for us with a note saying, '*Go raibh maith agaibh*.'

A week later, it was Sr Beatriz' feast day. We wrote '*Happy Feast Day St Beatriz*' in fat, curvy letters and drew flowers and plants, birds and bumblebees as she was the Botany teacher. It turned out absolutely beautiful. When we rushed out for break, Ev stayed behind to tie her shoe. When we all came back, we noticed one of the flowers had been turned into a beetroot. We looked at Evelyn.

"It's only a bit of craic," Eve said using the word Ricky used for saying *spraoi*.

On the way home, Kait got pensive and asked, "I wonder do the boys in the Brothers wish their teachers a happy feast day?"

"I can't imagine them writing nice things about any of the Brothers."

"Tomorrow, when we slope off to Wynn Shop to buy a Chester cake, I'll ask the lads from the Brothers if they do," Ev volunteered, only too delighted to have an excuse to talk to the lads.

As the months of the school year went by, we had become more daring and didn't stay in the yard during the first break. The convent gate was on Church Street, so we hopped across the street to Wynn's shop. Knowing Úna and Kait didn't get any pocket money, Ev and I pooled ours together to buy one large square of the rich, moist, current-y Chester cake, the same as the one Mammy bought for Daddy and Mr Delaney ate. We passed it around, holding the lardy, flaky pastry on the bottom and icing on the top by one finger and thumb.

"A few bites would fill an elephant," Ev would say. "I always get a desperate longing for it just before my periods." Which happened to us all. Our periods seemed to bring out the sweet tooth in us all.

The day after our chat wondering whether the boys decorated the board for the Brothers, we ran over to Wynn's and told Ev to find out if the tough boys wished their teachers a happy feast day. As we stuffed ourselves with buns, Ev went over to where the boys were to question them. When we looked over, we saw her taking a few pulls of one of the lad's cigarettes. The boys who hung around Wynn's were more into smoking than eating. She came back laughing. "They said the only thing they wished on any of the Brothers was to die roaring."

We had heard the older girls use the word 'crush.' We supposed that we were starting to get crushes on the boys too. We laughed and smiled over at the boys and wondered how the same boys, who not so long ago had been a pain in the neck, had become gorgeous and interesting. Now we spent hours talking about them. Kait was always sighing and writing Jim Smith's name on her arm and looking at it, touching it tenderly with her finger as though it were Jim himself.

"I feel a twitching in my mouth like a butterfly moving its wings when Jim Smith looks at me," Kait said.

"Everyone says Jim Smith is an awful yoke but he's as good as gold when he's near you, Kait, isn't he?"

"He is, so he is," said Kait. Moving airily like the fluff from a dandelion and gazing with her enormous green eyes, she knocked the wind out of all the boys. Their male gale-force toughness turned into a gentle breeze when they spoke to her. Jim Smith was no exception and we all thought he was in love with Kait. Evelyn had a crush on the stupid Ricky Martin with his big head full of himself.

"Well, I get the butterflies in my knees when I see Ricky. Ye don't know how my legs tremble whenever I catch a glimpse of him."

Her leg-trembling didn't stop her from being a devil though. When Ev saw Ricky's bike leaning against a shopfront, she would get us all to walk past it and she rubbed her hand against the handlebars, knowing it was the very spot his hands had touched. She said she got a thrill. I couldn't understand that because even though boys called after me when we were walking along the street, I never felt anything. If they raced past me on their bikes and whizzed back asking me if I wanted a lift home on the crossbar, I soon told them my legs were long and I could walk home. Ev was always telling me that such-and-such a one was crazy about me but while I liked talking to boys, me nor Úna never had the butterfly feeling that Ev and Kait said they felt.

Úna didn't have time for boys because she had to mind her brothers and sisters. Besides, the truth was boys didn't call after her. It might have been because her fuzzy, red hair never grew or got long like Evelyn's, who had curly hair too. Úna's mouth had gotten bigger, so her teeth didn't seem so long. She had curvy lips like Miss Walsh, the woman in the library who wore bright red lipstick. Úna's white skin with no freckles was translucent and dewy like a baby. She still wore specs and the big people said boys didn't like girls with glasses, so maybe that is why boys didn't mess with her like they did with the rest of us.

1967

We may have gone into first year as children, but we came out having bodies that were changing and moods that lasted as long as a chocolate bar between the four of us. That year of 1967 when we left our childhood behind, was a time when the news on the radio and television was as interesting to talk about as Legless shouting abuse at the bishop, another traveller family getting a house in Kilmartin Road, deciding if Jim Smith's eyes were the same shade as Paul Newman's, or if Ricky was as much in love with Ev as she was with him.

Places and people in The North and America were in everyone's mouth. Ian Paisley became part of the everyday gossip as though he were a local. He may have had a bigger, rounded type of head on him than the ones you'd see on the men around town, but people never shut up about him.

"If I had been near him, I know where the feicer's snowballs would have gone," Úna told us her father, Mr McNulty, said when he saw the news about Jack Lynch's car being snowballed in the North.

Kait's mother, Maisie Kenny, didn't care if Ian Paisley came down to Dublin and threw snowballs at all the TDs in the Dáil but she was affected badly by Elvis wedding, like my mother had been affected by Kennedy's assassination. Maisie was in so love with Elvis that, as well as going to all his pictures, she had a framed photo of him hanging up in the kitchen next to the Sacred Heart. Kait told us Maisie even tried to get their father to grow locks and have a quiff like Elvis. Mr Kenny's fringe of hair fell in his eyes long before the Beatles did, so it didn't matter how much Brylcrem he plastered on, he could never train his hair to go back. Now, after Elvis' wedding, sometimes Mrs Kenny seemed happy he had married Priscilla, saying she was a Galway-girl-type beauty, but other times she felt he had thrown himself away. We found it strange that a mother could be crazy about a singer. Mammy liked Frank Sinatra but spoke about him as if he was one of the priests.

"Frank sings that song beautifully," she'd say in the same tone she would use to say Father Mannion said Mass beautifully.

On television, we saw the American protest marches and heard Martin Luther King speaking at the rallies. Robert Kennedy was mentioned a lot, so Mr Delaney had to assure Mammy the anti-war protests wouldn't be anywhere near where Jackie lived and would not pester her and stop her from sleeping.

In the North, the Civil Rights Movement started too. We learned words like gerrymandering, squatting and water cannons. Mr McNulty, Úna's father, was saying we should all be up there helping the people fight the Brits. Daddy, on the other hand, said the ones in the North were bad enough on their own without getting ideas from the Blacks in America.

"But Daddy the Supremes are black, and they are beautiful. They wear lovely shiny dresses. Me and Ev want to learn to move and sing and dance like they do."

"Is Miss Canny's School of Irish Step Dancing not good enough for yis now?"

"Oh Dad! Don't be silly."

In the Odeon there was a gorgeous, black actor who was in all the films, like Troy Donohue and Rock Hudson used to be.

"Daddy we saw *Guess who's coming to dinner?* with Sidney Poitier last night. Me and Ev were saying if we invited a black person to dinner what would happen?" I never mentioned I was friends with Kait and Úna because I had an inkling he wouldn't like it.

"Well, if yis did, it would have to be the one on the Black Baby box."

"Daddy, I know there are no Black People in Drumbron but are there Black People in Dublin?"

"If there are, the colour must have washed off them with the rain."

"Maybe Dr Martin Luther King will come to Dublin like Jackie Kennedy is going to do."

"Wouldn't say so, he's busy with his dream."

"The first Martin Luther had a dream too and it came true."

"What do you mean?"

"We don't pay for indulgences now."

"Arlene lass, you have me there. What's that?"

"Before the rich could buy indulgences for their sins and get into heaven, but the poor couldn't cos they had no money."

"I thought Martin Luther was famous for nailing something to a door."

"Daddy! You know well he started the Protestant Church. Dr Martin Luther King is going to change things too."

"That man would be alright if he wasn't giving ideas to the young ones in the North."

"They aren't doing anything wrong, just saying it isn't fair a single woman gets a house before families with children do."

He looked sharply at me when I said that. I knew things others didn't know because when we were in Úna's house, Mr

McNulty told us the reasons why people were protesting in the North. I never told Daddy about the visits, and besides, he explained it to me in a different way.

"The authorities know what they are doing. We can't take sides without knowing the full facts." Whatever the facts were, the feelings of the people came out in songs that were played on the radio. '*The Black and Tan Gun*' became number one. Then everyone was singing '*The Merry Ploughboy.*' It made us four sing and hop around Úna's kitchen. Seeing us singing it prompted Mr McNulty to tell us about his father who fought in the War of Independence and how he went 'off to Dublin in the green.'

Jackie Kennedy's Visit to Dublin

Mammy and Mr Delaney, or Chester Cake Mouth as Ev started calling him, were talking about Jackie Kennedy's visit to Ireland. My mother was getting worried about what outfit she would wear for the day Jackie arrived and asked Mr Delaney's advice. Her wardrobe was full of shop-bought clothes because she didn't do any more sewing. The Singer sewing machine was banished to the press under the stairs.

"John, it's a great honour to have such an elegant and distinguished person as Jackie visit us," Mammy said.

Chester Cake Mouth replied, "My mother is over the moon we are going to Dublin to see Jackie and the two children, Caroline and John-John. She got the dentist to make her a pair of new teeth for the occasion."

Mammy didn't want to talk about Mrs Delaney's new teeth and quickly said, "John, we better stay the night. I don't want to be going around in circles like that time in March." In March they had driven up to see Tom Murphy's play, *The Famine*, with Mr Delaney's mother and her old set of teeth. They got lost coming back.

"Dervla, it wasn't my fault we got lost. It was that light that was in front of us that made me go off the main road."

I knew 'the light' wasn't Jack the Lantern. The villain with the light would not be so desperate to want someone like Mr Delaney and his mother to keep him company on his wanderings.

"John, you know as well as I do that it was your mother's fault we got lost."

"I don't know about that, Dervla. I'm still convinced it was the light that led me astray."

"It was your mother telling us that a sheep had her teeth in its mouth that got us lost," Mammy said. Daddy was behind the paper, reading it *mar dhea*, but before Mr Delaney went on the defence of his mother, Daddy managed to say quickly, "Dervla, there is a Wynn's Hotel in the city centre. Yis could stay there."

"There is no need for that," Mr Delaney said in a stern voice.

"Dervla can't go through another night of you taking wrong turns and ending up on a bog road."

"We were looking for my mother's teeth."

"Looking for her false teeth in the mouth of every sheep she saw," Daddy said in an amused voice but with an undertone of annoyance in it.

Mr Delaney defended his mother. "It wasn't her fault a dog frightened her."

"Frightened her so much she screamed, and her false teeth fell out. Thank God a squad car happened to be around," Mammy chimed in.

"I could have easily found the main road again without the squad car's help."

"Like you found your mother's teeth. How many hours were yis searching?"

"Not long. Once we looked under the back seat, Mother found them with no problem," Mr Delaney replied not realising Daddy was talking about them being lost on the road.

Mammy interrupted, "As I told William a hundred times, what a stroke of good luck we had. Imagine meeting a squad car on that road in the middle of nowhere after midnight. And the driver was so good. Remember John, when I told him I was Superintendent Blake's wife, he insisted on escorting us until we got near Drumbron."

What Mammy didn't know was that Daddy had told the Gardaí in Athlone to watch-out for a careful driver in a Morris Minor. He would be accompanied by a beautiful looking woman and another in a hat and fur coat. He gave them the licence plate number and the time he expected the car to go astray because from Dublin to Athlone, the road was straightforward but once across the Shannon, it was the wild west of twisty, stone-wall roads.

Mr Delaney was famous in Drumbron for his 'careful' driving since the time his car was crawling snail-pace in front of a funeral going through the town. The driver of the hearse had to get out and ask Mr Delaney to please get out of the way, so the corpse could get to the graveyard in time for his funeral.

The night they got lost and found was the night of Tom Murphy's play. While Mammy was sitting between Mr Delaney and his mother in the theatre, I was making the most of her absence and getting a fringe cut in my hair, like Sandie Shaw's, in the new hairdressing salon in Drumbron. Noreen had come from England and opened her salon near the Odeon Cinema in Merchant's Lane. We thought she had to be more 'with it' after living in England, even though she still wore her own hair in a beehive. I went to Noreen because I knew Peggy, who had set my hair for my First Holy Communion, wouldn't cut a rib of my hair without Mammy's permission, so that's why I grabbed my chance and got Evelyn to come with me to Noreen's.

At first when Mammy didn't appear, I was delighted, thinking she would not see my hair until morning, and I could go to bed without getting given out to. However, as the hours crawled by, I became as worried as Daddy who could not sit for long at the kitchen table. He kept getting up and going to the front door every few minutes.

When he saw the headlights of a car in the distance, he called me. We waited until the Morris Minor drew to a halt and Mammy got out. I rushed over to the car, desperate to wrap my arms around her neck but loud snores stopped me in my tracks. I approached the long, drawn-out sounds and saw they were coming from a fur hat in the backseat. In that split second, Mammy was walking away angrily while Mr Delaney called after her, "It was the light, Dervla, not me, that made us miss the turning."

I ran behind her to hug her but before I could, she saw my hair and ate the head off me, angrily telling me I looked a disgrace and I'd be lucky if she didn't chop it all off, leaving me bald as a sheared sheep. Daddy calmed her down and said she needed a cup of tea. I plodded up the stairs, the joy of seeing my mother arrive home safe and sound gone. She was taking her anger out on Daddy and letting him know he was bold for being away so much.

"Instead of being away in Belfast with the new Taoiseach, you should be at home with your family and taking me to the play."

Daddy had been promoted and had become some sort of a liaison officer and advisor in Dublin on matters in the North. He had been with Jack Lynch's team the time Ian Paisley had pelted the Taoiseach's car with snowballs. I felt like crying, but instead I thought of Mr McNulty and the funny thing he had said when he heard about the men throwing snowballs at the

Taoiseach's car. Mr McNulty had said, "I'd stick the biggest snowballs I could find up their arses so Jackeen could talk to Terence O'Neill in peace."

Second Year 1967-68

In September when we started second year, we were not the frightened gang of first years but girls who knew everything and needed to be with our friends more than we needed to be at home.

"Nuala, why are you always in a rush on Monday evening?" Ev asked Nuala, who was now part of our gang as she lived on a road near Úna's house and the two of them walked home together lots of evenings.

"It's to go to the Legion meeting in St Joseph's Hall. It starts a bit after half past seven."

"Are you in that place where all the Holy-Joes go?" Ev looked at Nuala as though she was mad.

I asked, "Is St Joseph's the parish hall on Barrack Street?"

"It isn't, Arlene. It's across from Supervalu near Castle Fields," Nuala explained. Then she turned on Ev, "Evelyn, don't you dare talk like that about the girls in the Legion. They are a nice bunch, and the meetings are not bad."

"How do you mean not bad?" Ev demanded to know, not bothered Nuala had given out to her.

"Well, I am out late instead of being stuck at home listening to my father telling me to shut the cross-door."

"Out late! How late?" shrieked Evelyn.

"How late?" Kait and Úna repeated, as interested as Ev who was leaning close to Nuala, wanting more details.

"Nine or half past nine."

"That late? Can we go?" Ev asked smiling and excited,

completely different from how she was a minute before when she was mocking the Legion.

"I suppose, but I don't know. Miss Kelly is in charge," Nuala said, surprised at the change, while Ev turned to us with glee in her eyes and told us, "Hey girls! We're joining the Legion."

"We have enough religion and holy stuff at school. I'm not joining." Úna didn't like Ev being the boss.

Then Ev explained it was so we could spend more time together, saying, "Girls, it's a way of staying out late without our mothers pestering us to know where we're going or who we are with."

Úna said, "Alright…" reluctantly but already convinced it was a good idea because she let Ev ask Nuala more details.

"Nuala, what time does the meeting start?"

"After the Rosary."

"What rosary are you on about?"

"The one that is said in the church."

"My mother goes to it," Kait informed us. "It starts at half past seven every evening."

"So that would mean sometime after eight o'clock. And what night is the Legion, Nuala?" Ev asked.

"Tuesdays."

"Hey, that means on Tuesdays we can hang around town talking until nearly ten without getting into trouble."

The Legion of Mary is a religious organisation whose members do good works in the community, but we joined to be able to stay out late.

At our first Legion meeting, we sat around a long rectangular table as quiet as Úna's little brother watching her unwrap a sweet for him, wanting to see what this Legion thing was all about. It started with a prayer, and then the secretary read the minutes of the last meeting. While she was reading, we studied the other women and girls to see what Ev had got us into.

Nuala and a few girls from her road, Tobair Benin's Road, were our age, but most of the others looked as old as our mothers. They had faded-looking faces as though they had been washed too often, and the newness was gone from them. A few had lips, but the others had only a line that opened like a mouth when they spoke. The slit was the sort of mouth gummy people have, so I was surprised to see there were teeth inside when they opened them to speak. Their voices were low and didn't go up and down like ours did when we talked.

The woman wearing the brightest clothes was Our Lady, hanging in the big picture in front, looking at us with her beautiful blue eyes and long lashes. Her lovely hands held each side of her heart. It was erupting in a small flame of fire with white roses wound around the middle part. If her eyes had been greener and her hair soft and blonde, she would have looked a bit like Kait, who also liked to wear cheerful colours.

The next item on the agenda was the Catholic papers delivered to families around town. Drumbron was big, so it was divided into different areas with three or four Legion members on each round.

Nuala and her friends had the round on the streets where the Home and the Home Babies used to be. They went to a house, handed in the paper and collected the money. The names and addresses were in a little notebook. In a ruled space after the name, a tick was put for paid and an x for not paid.

We were asked if we would like to help with the paper round. We said yes because everyone was looking at us, and we hadn't the nerve to say no. Miss Kelly told Mary O'Rourke and Cora Rushe to take us with them until we learned. After that, we would be able to do the paper round on our own.

Next, a list was drawn up of the members who would do an hour of adoration in the little chapel in Cork Road. We kept our heads down and lowered them even further to visit sick people in the Woods hospital.

The meeting finished with a prayer and Miss Kelly told us to be off home as we were young. The other members like Nuala and her pals stayed back to put away the prayer books and pamphlets, to count the paper money and to write the minutes. As we were leaving, Mary O'Rourke told us to meet her and Cora downstairs on Sunday at two.

As we left the grounds, we saw Jim and Ricky Martin smoking on the bridge over the small river that runs through Castle Fields. They called us over. We looked at each other, not believing how exciting joining the Legion was turning out to be. Ev strolled over and sat on the bridge as though this kind of thing didn't knock a flicker out of her. We followed her but drew back when Ricky offered us a pull of the fag he was smoking. Ev took it and put it to her lips, but we knew she didn't really know how to smoke. It was all pretence so Ricky would think she was big.

Kait asked Jim Smith, "What's that you're drinking? Is it orange-ade?"

"It isn't. Why don't you sit here?" he said, moving over a bit on the wall. Kait went to the spot, but instead of sitting down, she leaned her body over the wall and looked into the river.

"It's a bit late to go fishing now. All the fish are in bed saying their prayers," Jim said to her. We all laughed. Ricky then took over telling about how he had given a mouth of cheek to Brother Reilly when he asked why he hadn't his lessons done.

"The Christian Brothers?" Ev squealed as everyone in Drumbron knew they were animals and beat the pupils with a strap.

"Yup."

While we were taking in this shocking piece of information, Ev was asking him, "Do you really go the Brothers?"

"Ya, the auld fellow sent me there when they kicked me out of White Stones in Dublin."

"Were you expelled?" we said, amazed. We were talking to a boy who was so bold that he wasn't allowed to stay at school.

"What did you do?"

"Smoked, drank and told a few teachers to feic off. When I didn't pass my Inter Cert, the auld fellow went to speak to the headmaster about the quality of the teaching. To quote my father, 'The headmaster wasn't pleased and told me my son might do better at a different school.'"

"Do you like the Brothers?" Ev asked him.

"I do in my ar –" Before he finished the word, Jim gave him a puck and looked at Kait and said, "Pardon his French." We laughed.

"How long will you be in the Brothers?" Ev continued with her questions while Kait gazed into the river. Me and Úna kept quiet because we knew our friends had a crush on the two lads, and this was their chance to talk to them.

"I'm only there until I get into Pretoria College in Enniskillen. The auld fellow said it's the Irish that's holding me back, so he sending to the college some Oscar Wilde went to in the North, where they don't do Irish."

"Oscar Wilde!" Kait exclaimed.

"Ya, Oscar must be some big shot. The way Dad says the name you'd know he's important."

"My father went to that school, too," I said.

"I know, Mama told me."

Ricky's mother and my father were Anglicans and were sort of friends. Ricky's father was a TD. Mammy and Mr Delaney admired him, even though he was Fianna Fáil, the republican political party they hated. Any time Sean Lemass was mentioned on the radio or television they'd go mad because they disliked him and his name intensely.

"We are the laughingstock of the world. There we were last year celebrating the fiftieth anniversary of the Rising with a Taoiseach called Lemass and a President called De Valera and the country full of men with Irish names."

Mammy would be happy if she knew I was talking to a TD's son, but I wouldn't tell her because I didn't like Ricky Martin. Ev did and continued quizzing him.

"If you were in Inter Cert, you must be at least fifteen?" she asked Ricky.

"Older. The auld fellow made me stay back in sixth class cos he thought I wouldn't pass the Primary Cert."

"It's dead easy so why did he not let you do it?"

"Cos I was mitching and never at school. He sent me to St Colm's as a boarder for the year." Ev was looking at him with round eyes. A boy who could be in fifth year was talking to us who were only in second year.

Kait, who wanted to know everything about Jim but didn't want him to know she wanted to know, just said to him, "Are ye in the same class?"

"We are, but Ricky will be off to that place in the North soon."

At that moment, Úna pulled Ev off the wall and told us to duck down. "Look, the lights are gone out in the Legion room.

The gang of them will be coming out the door any second now," she said pointing to the upstairs window in St Joseph's Hall, "do we hide or make a run for it?"

"Run because if Miss Kelly see us, she'll tell our mothers we didn't go straight home." We started running with our bodies doubled down. The lads stayed where they were.

Ricky said, "Watch me give that auld Kelly wan notions."

"What are you doing to do?" We stopped to see what he was up to.

We tried to stifle our giggles when he said, "A bit of wolf whistling at her."

We doubled up in laughter when we saw Miss Kelly looking in the direction where the wolf whistles were coming from.

After that first meeting, the lads waited for us on the bridge most Tuesday nights.

The Paper Round

The following Sunday, we met Mary O'Rourke and Cora Rushe and did our first paper round, which was as easy as pie. At the next meeting, we told Miss Kelly we could do it on our own. She agreed because she needed Cora and Mary to visit some elderly women in the hospital. While the goody-goodies were visiting old people and looking at their wrinkly faces and gummy mouths, we were strolling along the street and chatting away. All we had to do was keep a lookout for the number of the house that a paper had to be delivered to. When we saw it, we ambled up the garden path, knocked on the door, spoke to the mother – the fathers never answered the door. We sort of played with the children who trailed and hid behind their mother's hip until they got to know us and stopped being shy.

Some houses had the money ready, others rooted around looking for it, and a few got the paper on tick. Mary O'Rourke had given us a little cloth bag with a string at the neck, a bit like the one Nan Gormley wore between her diddies, so we put the coins into it.

The only house Ev and me didn't want to go to was Mrs Maud Delaney, Chester Cake Mouth's mother. She lived in a big house at the end of Church Street, not far from the Fitzgerald's mansion. We begged Kait and Úna to go on their own up the long, windy, gravel path that crunched as they walked. Mrs Delaney answered the door and was very snotty with them, asking them their names and where they lived. When she heard Úna lived in Dun na Rí Road, she wanted to know if Úna was related to the McNulty man who had been in the Curragh.

"What did you tell her?"

"I acted stupid, pretending I didn't know what she was talking about."

"What's the Curragh anyway?" we asked her. Úna said it was the place where they had put the men like her father who wanted to fight for the people in the North. We still didn't know what it was or really care, besides Kait was saying, "That auld Delaney's one's son who goes to your house, Arlene, he gave my brother Seamus a lift one day he was on the road thumbing to Sligo. Seamus said he couldn't wait to get out of the car quick enough cos Delaney gave him the creeps."

"He gives me the creeps too every time I see him in my house. Hope he isn't there when I go home," I said.

"Are you not coming uptown so we can see what's on at the Odeon cinema?" Kait asked.

"A course I am, I think there's a Sandra Dee picture on. We could go and see it."

"I can't cos Mammy has no money. The small ones are sick, and Mammy bought Marietta biscuits to get them to eat."

I knew Úna and Kait didn't get pocket money like me and Ev did, so I said, "I was only codding about seeing Sandra Dee, sure I don't want to be stuck in the cinema on a lovely evening like today."

"You sound like an auld woman the way you're talking," Kait said but Ev backed me up.

"I want to be out too and not stuck in the cinema. We're only going to the Odeon to watch the people going in," said Ev. Like me, she had often heard her mother and mine and Mr Delaney's opinions about our friends. They gave out about people who had no money and how they thought they were keeping them. It was not true. The McNulty's and Kenny's had no money because the daddies didn't have a job.

"Our tax is paying for the school that McNulty man's children go to."

"Yes, John. What with free secondary schools now, it will be even harder to get girls to work in people's houses."

"They only have so many children to get the Children Allowance."

The Cinema

There were piles of people going in through the wide doors and up the marble steps to the ticket office to buy the yellow stubs from Miss Walsh. Her real job was in the library, but on Sundays and at night, she was caged in the little square room with glass windows on the landing at the top of the wide steps, selling tickets. It was bigger and much nicer than the train-seller's box room on the station, and Miss Walsh was nicer to look at than the man in the station with the peaked cap. She was glamorous like the ladies in the picture and even had an ashtray, with a cigarette balancing on the side in the booth. Ev liked to study her as she picked up the fag, in her finger with the long, red nails and put it between her lips to take a puff from it. She did this in between giving people tickets. Ev wanted to smoke like her because Miss Walsh was really as beautiful as a film star.

She had camel-coloured hair coming down to her shoulders and a big wave hiding half her face. Mammy said she copied her hairstyle from an actress called Veronica Lake, and it would be more in her line to cut it like Jackie Kennedy. Miss Walsh's eyebrows were gone and a thin, pencil circle, like a skinny rainbow with no colours, arched over her eyes. Her lips were pointy under her nose and as red as a cut on your finger.

When we saw Bonnie and Clyde in the Odeon, we thought Miss Walsh might be Faye Dunaway's sister or cousin and wondered if there was a handsome Warren Beatty waiting for her when she left the Odeon. My friends thought my father had an air of Clyde about him, only Dad's hair was blonde, and he didn't have a machine gun.

We knew Miss Walsh from the library in the town hall, the place where we borrowed books. She had long legs and was well-able to reach up to the top shelf to get the books we wanted. We knew this because our gang rushed into the library to the desk where she was sitting every Friday after school. First, we handed her the book we had borrowed the Friday before. She took it from us and placed a light brown slip of paper back into the small pocket on the front, inside page, which was stamped in lines of dates. Once she had the borrowed book registered as returned, we moved slowly around the long shelves looking for the book we wanted to read that week. We never made any noise because when we were small, she had given out to us for running and talking, and we still remembered how shamed she had made us feel. Even Ev didn't give her a smart answer. It might have been because she was different with the make-up and the smoking, which was a very daring thing for a woman to do in Drumbron.

That Sunday of our paper round, when we got to the cinema, Jim and Ricky were on the path in front of the Odeon, smoking. They called us over and started bragging about how they could get into the pictures for free. We moved in close to listen. Even though we had said we would rather be outside on the lovely, sunny evening, we really wanted to see Sandra Dee.

"How do ye do it? Sure Miss Walsh has eyes like a hawk," Úna said.

"I won't tell ye unless you promise to give me a kiss tonight," Ricky said, looking at Ev.

"A kiss in the ar, is what I'll give you," Ev said. We laughed as we were used to her saying 'ar' instead of arse like the lads said.

"I'd love to see Sandra Dee," Kait was saying, "I love the way her ponytail swings from side to side. She smiles with the dimples near her mouth."

Jim had the name of a hard lad around town, but when he looked at Kait, he had a glazed, glassy look in his eyes. "You smile with dimples too."

"Are you getting feicing romantic, ya eejit," Ricky said pushing Jim.

"I amn't. I'm just saying you don't have to be American to have dimples. Come on, let's do what we have to do, or the picture will be over by the time we slope in."

They peeped in the door and said, "Your wan is putting her coat on. That means she's leaving." Jim ordered us to back around the corner, out of sight. We did so with Ricky holding Ev by the waist as though she needed help. "Wait there quietly until I hear her come out." The door opened and shut. Jim greeted Miss Walsh, "Howya." She didn't answer.

We heard her steps trailing off down the street. Jim appeared and moving his hand like the soldier in charge does in the war films, he urged us to file in through the door one by one, his face telling us to be quick about it.

Signalling to the speckled marble-looking steps, he indicated we had to scale them. We obeyed, barely breathing and casting sideways and upward glances, afraid Miss Walsh would loom in front of us, demanding to know what we were doing like the day in the library when we were small.

Jim had pulled open the heavy door that went into the long dark corridor and ordered us through it. He waited until we were safely on the other side of the door before he came in and closed it quietly.

Standing at the side of the line we had formed, he whispered behind his hand that we had to slither to the end of the corridor and wait at the door. It was the entrance to the rows of seats people called 'the gods.' They were cheaper than the stalls.

We weren't to budge an inch until he returned. Ricky wasn't taking heed of him because he kept trying to kiss Ev. She was pretending to push him away but falling against him and giggling. While the two were acting the eejit, we were imagining and whispering all the things that could happen to Jim.

"I betcha Francie the Torch saw him sneaking in and called the Gardaí," Úna said while I thought it was so dark Jim would fall and hit his head against the wall. Then Ricky stopped messing with Ev for a minute and frightened us by saying, "There's a crowd from Kilmartin Road who wanted to beat Jimbo up."

"Why would they want to do that?" Kait asked in a quivering voice.

"Cos he wouldn't give them the old tyres from his father's garage last year for the bonfire."

"That's not true, so it's not," Kait wailed, really worried about the boy she was going to marry.

"It is. Wait until you see how he comes out with half his teeth missing."

"No, Francie the Torch will hear them and save Jim," Kait said, assuring herself he would be fine.

"He won't, cos Francie sleeps through the whole matinee," Ricky said to make sure she stayed worried.

"He doesn't."

"He does."

"Why would he sleep and miss the pictures?" Kait asked, surprised, as nobody in their right mind would waste time sleeping instead of watching the film.

"He's conked out. Who do you think cleans this place every night? Miss Walsh?"

"I know she doesn't, but why would Francie sleep and miss Sandra Dee?" Kait still wasn't convinced.

"It's the only chance he gets to sleep. Didn't you know his auld wan snores? The neighbours say they can hear her in their houses, so Francie sleeps here when he can."

Kait made a sound like a sob, frightened for Jim. At that very moment, her hero returned. He said Francie the Torch was asleep in the back row, so that we could slope in, but it still meant we had to be careful because Francie might wake up if we made noise.

"Now, crouch down and follow one another in a line to the first row. Sit in the seats slouched down for a while.

Ev, who had pushed Ricky away *mar dhea*, demanded to know. "Why?"

"Because the ones behind have got to get used to seeing bulks in front of them. Then straighten up little by little."

Sandra Dee's beautiful perky face smiling at Troy Donahue welcomed us to our first free matinee.

Jim and Ricky weren't looking at the screen at all. They had their heads turned around, looking at the sparkly glow from the cigarettes of the lads they hung out with. Jim took a swig from a naggin bottle, like the ones Mick the Sticks drank from and passed it to Ricky. They left us and sloped back to sit by the lads with the fags. We didn't care because now we knew how to get into the pictures for free.

On the way home, Ev said she wanted to go to Wynn's Shop. Without even asking us, she put her hand into the bag with the string and took out a coin. Before our astonished eyes, she handed the money to Mrs Wynn and asked for a choc-ice. She walked out of the shop with the beautiful, brown covered white ice cream on a stick held before her face. The three of us moved closer to each other, forming a semi-circle and looking at her, not believing she had taken money from the bag to buy a choc-ice.

"Ev, you took money from the Legion bag," Úna gave out to her as though Ev were her little sister.

"So?" Ev answered.

"Ev, that's stealing," Kait told her in a cross voice.

"A course it isn't. Do ye want a bite?" she said to Úna, holding the choc-ice in front of her face.

"I don't," Úna said.

"Me neither," Kait said.

"Me neither three," I said.

"Ev, we have to give all the money to Miss Kelly on Monday night."

"Sixpence? Sure, that's nothing," she said. We heard that beautiful cracking sound the hard chocolate coating made as her teeth broke into it and saw the fine, spider web lines spread around the bite.

"It's my turn now," I said, trying to take the choc-ice from her, but Úna got there before me. In total, we got about three bites each but took turns licking the stick until the ice cream wrapped around the wood was gone. It was worth the sin on our soul for eating stolen goods.

"Where will we get the money to put back in the bag?" Úna wanted to know.

"We don't have to put it back," Ev said.

"We do, it's not our money."

"We don't, cos if we cross out this name here of Miss Flynn, we can say we only sold fourteen papers and that way we have enough money."

"But we sold fifteen papers."

"I know, *amadán*, but Miss Kelly doesn't know that. We always get extra papers in case a new person wants to buy some, don't we?"

"We do but what are you trying to say?"

"It means there isn't an exact amount of papers to sell to the exact same amount of people every week."

"I don't know what that means, so I don't," wailed Kait.

"Miss Flynn will tell on us," Úna said.

"She won't. She's too old to go out and if we are nice to her, she'll be happy to see us."

"But if we cross out her name, we won't have a paper to give her," Úna calculated.

"A course we will. Amn't I after telling ye we get extra copies of the newspaper. So we'll give one of those to Miss Flynn every week and she'll pay us with no bother."

It seemed complicated but Ev was right. Miss Kelly never noticed. To make up for involving Miss Flynn in our scheme, even though she didn't know what we were doing, we spent plenty of time talking to her about what was on the news, like the death of the three Apollo crew members and when we asked her about it, she said, "More in their line to keep away from the Moon. Sure what would they be they wanting up there anyway?" I told her my mother was hoping Jackie Kennedy wouldn't be too affected by the three deaths and started wearing black. "Jackeen Kennedy. Is your mother a Kennedy?"

"She is one of the Kennedy's from Roscommon," Ev answered, delighted Miss Flynn didn't know who delivered the paper and thought we were Kennedys from Roscommon, but Kait was worried we were committing a sin and wanted to go to confession.

"Kait, don't for the life of you go to Fr Mannion. Wait until we go to Galway in the car with your uncle and confess it there cos the priests don't know you," Ev explained to her.

"It's only a venial sin, so we still can go to Communion, and no one will know we have a sin on our soul," I said, thinking three bites out of a choc-ice wasn't worth confessing. It was like me taking sugar from the bowl in the kitchen when I was small.

"Sure, it's not a sin not to write someone's name in a book. We didn't take the sixpence from Miss Flynn's purse or anything like that," Ev reassured her.

"You're right, missing Mass is a real big sin, and you can go to hell. Hitting someone or giving cheek doesn't get you sent to hell," Úna added to keep Kait from worrying too much.

"Or buying a choc-ice," Ev added.

Mass On Sunday

On Sundays, I went to Mass with Mammy in the car. While she was parking, I kept my hand on the handle and as soon as the car stopped for a second, I had the door opened and slid out as quick as I could. She used to call after me in an exasperated whisper, but I pretended I didn't hear her and hurried over to the smaller side door on the convent side where my pals were waiting. We went into Mass together. Mammy walked to the wide, double-door entrance in the front of the building, smiling and nodding to people but mad inside at me for having gotten away. She told Daddy I didn't stay with her at Mass.

"Arlene, what's this about you not staying with Mammy in the chapel?" he asked me. Knowing Mammy would tell-tattle to Daddy, I had my excuse ready. I convinced him I didn't sit with Mammy because I needed to know every corner of the church as I was writing an essay about the chapel and its layout. It was half true because every year at school there was a prize for the best written essay on a building in Drumbron. To make the story fully true I asked Mrs McLoughlin to tell me about the chapel. She had learned all the details about the chapel when her American cousin came on holidays and had enquired about the fine church building.

Thanks to Mrs McLoughlin, I can describe the place of worship with my eyes closed. It was built during the Famine. The people of Drumbron and in the countryside were dying on the sides of the road with green juice coming out of their mouth, but still, money was collected to build the Gothic-style church.

There are five entrances for public use and one for the clergy. The most important one is the big, double, wooden, panelled door set in the middle at the front of the church, the one that Mammy uses. The two smaller ones at each side of the main door are the entrances to the narrower areas where the confession boxes are. Kait and Úna's mammies sit in that part. Towards the back, at the edges of the hands of the crucifix structure are two more doors. These two side-doors are the favourites of the old people. Maybe it is because there are only a few pews, and they don't have to walk a long way up the aisle to receive communion. At the very back, behind the altar and sacristy, there is the private door for the use of the clergy and altar boys.

On the inside of the principle, double entrance there is an antechamber that Mrs McLoughlin called the vestibule. It is a wide space with stained glass windows on each wall letting light in. Two round-bellied, one-legged holy water fonts stand guard on each side of the heavy, wooden doors like soldiers reminding people to dip their fingers into water, bring the wet surface to their foreheads, stomach and shoulders and make the sign of the cross before entering the sacred place. A bit in from the fonts, there is a lacy-golden table with candles on it for those who want to put a penny into the slot and light a candle before going into the real part of the chapel. It is always there on the left-hand side, while the table with two men sitting at it is only there on Sunday. The men have a basket on the table in front of them and their eyes oblige people to drop money into it before entering the grand chamber.

Nearly hidden away to the side, there is a narrow, dark door, behind which is a cork-screw stairs going up to the choir-loft. This gallery is like a balcony overlooking the central aisle, where the choir members stand and praise the Lord in hymns. Their voices rise to the ceiling before dropping onto the congregation in the pews below. The voices, made even more wonderous by the organ music accompanying them, reach every corner and fill the church with a heavenly sound. The deep, lingering notes of the organ wrap their vibrating sound around the walls and corners of the chapel even to the enclosed, tiny, horizontal hallway packed with men who aren't keen to be seen. The big boys who complain they only attend Mass because the 'auld wan' made them go, also gather in this no-man's-land between the antechamber and the nave. Most of the 'don't want to be seen' men never enter the main body of the church until the day they are carried up the central aisle to in front of the altar inside a coffin.

The stained-glass window behind the altar allows the sun to light up the wide central aisle. Pillars, that Mrs McLoughlin calls buttresses, hold up the lofty roof and separate the pews and people in the central aisle from the two narrow aisles on each side. Winging out from the top of the church, where the main altar is, are two side chapels, like short arms that go off to the left and to the right. They each have their own altars, pews and doors.

Me and my friends used the side door and sat with the old people because we could talk better there and not because I was studying the chapel to be able to describe it for my essay, as I told Daddy.

Still and all, my half-truths did me no harm because I won the best essay prize with my composition, 'The Church in Our Town.' After that, I had no excuse not to sit with Mammy in the central aisle until the sodality of Our Lady saved me.

Sodality of Our Lady

Towards the end of second Year Cora Rushe came into our class and told us about the school sodality. Fingering the silver medal she was wearing around her neck, she explained how in Leaving Cert, some girls had the privilege of wearing Our Lady's medal when they became Children of Mary. Joining the school sodality was one of the ways we could prove we were worthy of the honour that would be bestowed on us that great day.

"What is the school sodality, Cora?" I asked as I felt I knew her from the Legion.

"Girls who commit to attending Mass and receiving Communion every Sunday."

"My mother wouldn't let me miss Mass for anything in the world," Mary O'Rourke said.

"Sure, we always go to Mass too," Ev added.

The nun could see we were taking over the discussion from Cora and swiftly intervened saying, "Naturally, we wouldn't expect any less. However, now that you are becoming young ladies, we feel you may need safeguards from the many temptations that you will meet, so joining the School Sodality and going to the prayer meetings in St Joseph's Hall on Wednesday nights are some of the ways we would recommend."

"Is it in the same hall as the Legion of Mary?" Evelyn asked, knowing well it was but letting us know it was where we met Jim and Ricky after the Legion.

"As a matter of fact it is."

"Then I want to join," Ev affirmed.

"Very well. We need girls like you, Evelyn Curry."

"My friends will join too," added Ev, letting us know that we were joining whether we wanted to or not.

"Naturally, their names, along with the rest from the class, will be written in this book as members of the Sodality," the nun said and Cora held up a slim, narrow, hard-covered book with a gold tassel on a gold thread. "The girl I elect to be in charge of this book will note the absence of any girl from Mass or those that arrive late."

Ev ducked under the desk to tie her shoe and Úna, Kait and me lowered our heads so Cora or the nun couldn't meet our eye. Mary Cosgrove was picked, so until we did our Leaving Cert, Mary had the job of checking to see if girls in the sodality were in time for Mass.

The School Sodality made my Sundays fun as it meant I didn't have to sit with Mammy anymore. I met my friends at the side door, gushing about all the exciting things that had happened since we had seen each other the previous evening. Then we made our way to the middle pews on the right-hand side of the central aisle, still whispering and looking across at the boys who sat on the left-hand side of the aisle, in their Sodality. We spend the whole Mass giving sideway glances over to the lads on the other side and commenting on their good and bad aspects as we 'spotted the talent.'

"That guy is gorgeous."

"You can say that again."

"Is that fellow with the green jumper the one that's going out with Nuala?"

"No, she's going with the fellow behind him," said Ev, who had a crush on Ricky Martin. She spent Mass spotting the talent too, even though she insisted she only did it for me and Úna, as we needed to be fixed up with a fellow before we went into Inter Cert. We knew Ricky fancied Ev because after the

Legion meetings, he was always on the bridge in Castle Fields and one evening called Ev 'frisky' and kissed her. Ev couldn't help but act the eejit and one Monday evening after the Legion, she stood on the wall beside Ricky and pretended to fall off.

"Catch me, Ricky! I am Nelson getting blown off the pillar!" she said, singing the new song that was always on the radio.

Up went Nelson in Old Dublin,
Up went Nelson and the pillar too.

When Ev jumped off, Ricky caught her. She was tiny and he was well able to hold her over the river as though he was going to throw her into it.

"Ricky, it's not fair, I want to scream but you know well I can't cos old Miss Kelly is still upstairs," she said pointing to the light in the window in St Joseph Hall.

"I'm not letting you go until you feicing well scream and frighten your wan from the Legion," Ricky told her. She started to giggle and to stop the laughter from escaping, she stuck her fist in her mouth. When he let her go, she leapt at him, but he moved away on his long legs, dodging her easily. He stopped when he saw her hand and stepped in close.

"Hey, your hand is all red. Look at the teeth marks on it. I'd better kiss it better." That was the first kiss Ev got from Ricky. We knew they would end up going out together, even if she helped us spot the talent in the chapel.

After Mass, I stayed with my gang on the convent side of the church until I saw Mammy getting into the car. I'd run to the car, and we went home for dinner or 'lunch' as Mammy had started calling it after she became Gay Byrne-ised. One Sunday eating the shop-bought chicken, I said, "Mammy, do you remember when I was small, and you used to crock the hens and hang them up on the backdoor." She got really cross as she didn't want to remember those times.

"Mary, I don't like you using vulgar words. Please don't say 'crock' ever again. You are fourteen, so start behaving like a young lady."

"But I behave like a good girl. I'm in the Legion and the Sodality."

"That may well be, but young ladies play tennis, not the accordion. I wonder what your Aunt Hazel will make of you playing it when you spend time with her this summer."

"I know she'll like it."

"Aunt Hazel will not like it," Mammy said with such certainty in her voice that I had to put her right.

"Mammy, there is marching band in Daddy's town with accordion music and everybody said the band is fantastic, even Aunt Hazel."

"Nonsense," she insisted.

She was not going to be convinced so I said, "In July, they have a big parade in the town. I could play my accordion and march with the band when I'm there, couldn't I? Daddy and Aunt Hazel wouldn't stop me?"

Daddy put his hand on the top of my head and was about to tousle my hair when Mammy said, "Over my dead body. There is no way a daughter of mine is walking down the middle of the street playing an accordion. Do you want people to think we are related to Jock Connor?" Daddy withdrew his hand and ducked behind his newspaper. He knew he had to handle her with care because since Robert Kennedy had been killed at the beginning of June, Mammy was down in the dumps sometimes and at others she'd flare up for the least thing. She was worrying about Jackie and Daddy worried about her.

On account of that conversation about the accordion-playing, Mammy convinced Daddy that I should play tennis like all young ladies do.

I ended up going to the Castle Fields to play tennis. Ev came along with me because Ricky was always mitching school and hanging around Castle Fields and it would be her chance to see him. Ev told me any time she saw Ricky, her heart was like a ball hit by a tennis racket. It slammed against her chest and kept spinning back and forward.

"You're mad, Ev," I said

"No, it's true. When I see him, my body goes crazy? There is a lovely tickle in my throat. I never noticed I had a mouth before unless it got burned with hot tea, but now when I see him it comes alive. I feel it warm and tingly. My lips nearly leave my mouth, they want to fly over to his. Oh, Arlene, it's lovely because it's something I never felt before."

"I still think you are away with the fairies."

"When you grow up and fall in love, you'll know."

"Ev, I'm fourteen and you're only a year older than me."

"Shut up. There he is," she said casting her eyes in the direction of the bench that was outside the high metal netting that cut the tennis courts off from the rest of the park. I looked and she got mad.

"Don't let him see you looking," she said but I looked anyway. Ricky's long legs were sprawled along the front of the bench because he was tall and really handsome like Rock Hudson with dark hair and blue eyes. He was wearing beige slacks and a white shirt and a blue jumper with a white stripe going through the V-neck, like the ones Troy Donoghue wears in the films, was thrown over his shoulders, with the sleeves hanging down in front.

"What are you going to do, Ev? Will I wave over at him?"

"No. I'm going to hit the ball out, so he picks it up and gives it to me."

Instead of playing tennis, Ev shot the balls outside the metal fence. Ricky stood up and caught the ball in the palm of his hand, walked over to the fence and handed them back to Ev. They said a few words and then did the same stupid acting-the-eejit thing again. When he went back to the bench the second time, Ev whispered to me that Ricky was the bees' knees. Plenty of other girls were after him and she was lucky he was taking notice of her. I thought she was silly to be love with a such a horrible boy, a right bully. He used to mock Seán, Tom and Kevin, the boys we knew from the river, about their clothes and shoes all the time.

The first time he mocked them, they told him to "Feic off with your mop of curly hair!" All the 'with-it' boys wore their hair falling down on their forehead like the Beatles. Ricky's hair was curly and wavy, and it wouldn't stay in a fringe. He was so mad he punched Kevin in the face and lashed a kick at Seán. Kev hit him back, but Ricky growled he'd tell his father to get the Gardaí after them. Kev backed off. He knew Ricky's father was a TD and had 'pull' with the Gardaí.

Ev thought her curly-haired boy was great and she smiled like a Cheshire cat when he boasted about how he behaved at board-school. The more Ev listened to Ricky and the awful things he said, the more she fell in love with him.

Kait was in love with Jim Smith because he was good and went to Mass. He smoked and stayed outside in the long, glassed-in-space with the men who didn´t want to be seen. That way he could be popping in and out all the time for a fag.

When Kait went to the altar rails to receive communion, her knees made her walk wobbly, because she could see Jim looking at her as she came down to her seat. Once, he told her the only reason he got up out of bed, at eleven on a Sunday the morning, was to see her bum.

"I nearly had kittens, so I did, and I felt my face going red. I'm sure I looked terrible because even though red suits me it doesn't look good on my face," Kait told us.

Of the two, I liked Jim better. He was handsomer than Ricky and had lovely dewy skin like Elvis Presley and his lips were fatty. Still and all, I didn't like Kait being so in love with him because Mr Delaney told Mammy that the Fitzgeralds and the Smiths were great friend and that he would not be surprised if there wasn't a match made between their children. He knew everything, such as Loretta was at the prestigious Glenmore Abbey in Connemara mixing with the elite. I didn't care where she was, but towards the end of first year, I saw her wearing a beautiful red blazer with gold buttons and a black pleated skirt and patent shoes at Sunday Mass and felt a pinch of jealousy because Mammy would never allow me to wear a red cardigan, don't mind a red blazer with gold buttons.

Úna and me thought our two pals were nuts because, like me, her knees never shook at the sight of a boy. We knew we would never want to kiss them and get their spits in our mouths. When Ev told us Ricky had put his tongue into her mouth, we felt like vomiting. It was such a disgusting thing to do. If any boy put their dirty old tongue into my mouth, I'd bite it off. It was fun looking at them sitting on the other side of the chapel or slagging with them when we were on our way to study but that was enough. Even when I skipped attending study, I was in more of a mind to go up Clonthu Hill to see Nan Gormley than go to the Castle Fields to talk to the boys.

Study Time

We had study from five to seven so we couldn't go up Clonthu Hill as much as before unless we mitched study and besides, Nan Gormley wasn't well in herself and had taken to her bed.

"I amn't in the humour for talking since Mick the Sticks was taken off to Ballinacora."

"Will we make you tea?"

"Do and make yerselves a drop. Sit there by the fire, there's sure to be a bit of the pudding Catherine Maynee made."

I was asking, "Who's Catherine Maynee?" while Ev said, "Why did they take Micks the Sticks away?"

"For joining in on the carols before the organ started and still singing long after it finished."

"Was he singing at Midnight Mass, Nan?" Úna asked.

"He was. The poor cratur drank too much and went up to the chapel wanting to say a prayer for the souls of those people from India who died in that plane accident."

"The plane that crashed into the sea?"

"That's right. He said the Banshee is around these nights wailing on account of the deaths."

"She isn't, Nan. You know well she only comes before someone dies not after," I said but saw straight away she didn't want the Banshee mentioned and she started talking about Mick the Sticks again.

"He caused an awful ruckus with his singing. I heard there was more laughing in the church than at the Christmas funny play they put on in the parish hall."

While we were there, a boy who Nan said was Catherine Maynee's Michael came in to see if Nan needed anything. Ev called him 'a fine yoke' in a whisper to us. He was tall and straight and had a dimple in his chin. Even though his head was miles up on a strong neck, his straw-coloured hair and sky-blue eyes reminded me of Liam, the little Home baby. I was surprised Liam came into my head because even though I sometimes woke up from a dream that Liam was in, I never thought about him when I was awake. Catherine Maynee's Michael was surprised to see visitors and said he call back later.

"That young buck has a heart of gold. Calls in every day to see how I am."

"Who is he? I've never seen him around town," Ev said.

"His mother is one of the lot of itinerants who got those empty houses in Kilmartin Road."

"Who got my Uncle Martin's house, do you know?"

"*Thrath*, you have legs on you that can walk and a mouth on you that can talk, so if anyone should know, it's you and not me, a girleen."

The next night when we were with Ricky and Jim on the wall after the Legion meeting. Ricky was singing Joe Dolan's *Pretty Brown Eyes* to Ev when Catherine Maynee's Michael crossed over Castle Fields. He stood in front of Úna and told her he wanted to talk to her. Ricky shouted at him.

"What do you think you're doing, Stiff Neck?"

Michael didn't answer him because he was saying to Úna, "Your Da asked me to come and get you."

Ricky was off the wall coming towards Michael.

"But why?" Úna was asking.

"You are needed to stay with the young ones."

"Why am I at this time of night? Sure, the children are in bed?"

"Your ma and da have things to do."

"What things?" Michael looked down and was going to answer but Ricky was in front of him and pushed Michael away, so we barely heard the words 'washing the corpse.'

"Whose corpse?" Úna asked. Before he answered, we all knew who the Banshee had been crying for. Nan was dead.

Ricky was still talking, saying, "You knac–" when we heard an almighty slap that sounded like a thunderclap in the quiet of the night.

Kait had walloped Ricky across the face. Jim Smith's eyes and mouth were wide open. Kait was crying and shaking her hand. We pulled her towards us and the three of us walked away from the two boys with Michael following behind us.

"Don't go anywhere with that tinker, do ye hear?" Ricky roared after us.

Kait turned back and said, "You keep your gob shut or I'll bust it for you, you ignorant pig. How dare you talk like that when Úna's grandmother is dead?"

The Wake

Nan was to be waked in her house with money she had been saving for years in the pouch. I remembered how she had given me a tuppence coin from it when I made my First Holy Communion. Relatives were coming from England and Scotland and the ones from Ireland were already in Drumbron. I was determined to go to Nan's wake but I would have to slope out of my house so Mammy wouldn't see me. I'd also heard my father saying to Garda Curry, "Gerry, the McNulty's are fierce Republicans and God knows who'll turn up for the wake. They might use the funeral as a cover for something else."

"Ah, but still and all, I don't think they'd have the nerve to use the funeral for a meeting."

"With all that going on up the North, we can't be too careful. Have the men check who's going in and out of the house but discreetly. We want no disrespect."

"If the tricolour…"

"If they want to, let them drape the coffin in the tricolour, no good causing trouble for that."

Knowing I could be recognised, I put on the old cardigan Mrs McLoughlin kept in our house. Taking a black handbag from Mammy's room, I shoved the scarf I had found in the laundry basket into it and left our house. I ran through Kilmartin Road and just before I turned the corner to go up Clonthu Hill, I put on the scarf and pulled it well down on my forehead and tied it like the old women do. Then I stuck the black handbag under my oxter. Stooping my shoulders down to seem smaller, I hoped I looked like a friend of Nan's as I walked towards the cottage.

The place was crowded. Everyone was there, even the ones who were too sick or too old to venture outside their doors came to pay tribute to Nan. Úna later said Nan would love to have been at the wake to see the great send-off she got.

When I got well into the kitchen, where Nan was laid out, I took off my disguise and went over to say goodbye to my Nan who was laying in the coffin, her rosary beads entwined between her fingers. Looking at her, the tears that had been making my eyelashes blink, fell. I didn't try to stop them. My lovely Nan was gone.

I loved Nan like she was my own grandmother.

I loved Nan because she was the guide who led me to a wonderful world of magic and fairies, to an invisible realm that existed alongside the world we see every day.

I loved Nan because she brought me back in time to when the Big Hunger was causing people to die on the side of the road with their mouths green from eating grass.

I loved Nan who told me of people who survived the Titanic and came back and told her of those who didn't and described how the unfortunates died in the icy waters of hell.

I loved Nan because she was my teacher, telling me stories about the Celtic civilisation with its customs and culture.

I loved Nan because she loved the language of her youth and told me to hold it dear and not let it be destroyed or rooted from our souls.

I loved Nan because she told me the names of the families around Drumbron who took the soup and how it had poisoned them and their descendants, making them heartless and envious of the ones who hadn't taken it – the ones who had stayed true to what was theirs and their forefathers.

I loved Nan for talking about the laws from centuries ago when women were nearly as good as men.

I loved Nan for being a woman with no shame or secrets, speaking of Jack and how he was so handsome and the joy they shared in coming together and the delight a man can bring to a woman's body.

I loved Nan for not hiding from me the terror the Black and Tans had inflicted on people. She told me she was in Tuam in June and saw the burning of the town hall, even though Tuam was a garrison town.

Nan gave me pride in being a woman. I knew I could be a soldier like she was, a woman who loved a man with no shame, a holder of a things from the past, a teacher, a *seanchaí*, a caretaker of the less fortunate, a strong but kind person.

As the night wore on, my tears turned to joy and pride as people remembered and praised her as though she were a chieftain of old. They spoke about how she had brought food and tea, in a bottle, to the men in the fields when they were fighting the Black and Tans, often going hungry herself to feed the men on the run.

For the people present, Nan was as important, if not more, than John F Kennedy and other high and mighty people. Prince, her dog, stood by the coffin. When people finished speaking about Nan, he would howl-bark as though he agreed.

Jock Connors, who was too frail to play in *An Lár*, was there. Michael Stiff Neck had carried the accordion to Nan's house so Jock could play Nan's favourite tunes. I asked him if I could play *The Wearing of the Green* on his accordion. People sang the words while I played. It was one of Nan's favourites. I got a rousing round of applause and Úna asked me to play it again and she sang, *The Rising of the Moon* to it, as the air for the two songs was the same.

I forgot about my plans for going home early and stayed until Prince came over to me, sent by Nan, I suppose to remind me I had to leave. After patting his head, I put my scarf and cardigan back on and left.

The next evening me, Ev and Kait missed study to go to the removal. We linked our arms in Úna's and followed in the fifth row of mourners behind the hearse, me with my head low in case Dad was watching. As it was nearly dark, I didn't think he'd see me.

The next day we didn't walk behind the hearse. We waited in the cemetery until the coffin was brought to the grave and watched as the priest sprinkled the holy water on it and recited the rosary for the repose of Nan's soul.

Nan was Úna's grandmother, but I loved her as though she were mine. My mouth and throat were tight when I thought she was gone from the house, and I would never see her again. Prince must have been feeling the same because Úna told us the dog was walking around the outside of the house with his head hanging nearly on the ground. Michael tried to get the dog to go with him to his house, but Prince barked at him, so he left him there, bringing him food and water every few days. Less than a week after Nan's wake, Michael found Prince dead.

Life went back to normal with Ricky his normal hateful self when we met him and Jim after the Legion. He started mocking Michael, calling him 'Stiff Neck' cos he walked really straight.

He said we had to sing Val Doonican's *Walk Tall Walk Straight & look the world right in the eye* anytime we saw Michael. I told Ricky to sugar off, but he only laughed and said I had a crush on the itinerant boy.

"If she does, so what," Kait said, "Michael looks like Troy Donoghue and you're jealous of him, so you are."

The Pioneers
At the end of second year, the Reverend Mother came into our class to tell us about The Pioneers. She explained people took a vow to renounce drink for the rest of their lives. They wore a pin so everyone could see they were giving up drink for the glory of God. She asked if we had any questions.

"Is the pin free?" Kait asked.

"No. It costs a shilling."

"When do we take the pledge and become a Pioneer?" Cora Rushe asked.

"Next Sunday after the last Mass."

I told Mammy and Daddy about the Pioneers. Mammy was a Pioneer but never wore her pin because she said it clashed with the string of pearls she wore around her neck. Sometimes she had a tiny glass of sherry which she didn't consider drinking as she was imitating Jackie, who also had a drink every now and then. She thought it was a wonderful idea for the young people to take the pledge, but Daddy didn't.

"Dervla, the wee lass is too young to be making promises. Let her wait until she is older and decide for herself what she wants to do," Dad said winking at me.

"William, I don't want Mary to be the only girl in her class who doesn't take the pledge."

"The idea that a child should make a sacrifice to atone for the sins of others is ridiculous."

"William, you don't understand."

"You, above all people, are telling me that I don't understand that people make sacrifices to please others."

"William, I'm just saying people will talk about Mary if…"

"People are always going to talk about Arlene because she is such a beauty."

"William, precisely because she is such a good-looking girl, we have to be more careful. If she doesn't take the pledge, before we know it, she will have a bad name."

"The only one people talk about in this town is Legless. He was up shouting at the Bishop again. The stay in Ballinacora didn't do him any good."

"William, don't change the subject. Mary has to take the pledge."

Daddy's face got stiff and in his Garda voice he said, "Enough. In the summer we are going to my sister's. She'll be having dinner parties and I am not saying to Hazel my daughter won't have wine because the Catholics make children take pledges." That was the end of it. Mammy didn't say another word.

That year there were two girls who didn't become Pioneers, me and Úna.

Mr McNulty said, "Tell that long-faced nun that the 1916 leaders didn't fight to free Ireland so the feicing church can stop people from drinking."

Úna hadn't the nerve to say it to the Reverend Mother because the whole town knew Mr McNulty himself liked to drink. He said he only went into Quinn's shop and pub on *An Lár* to make sure Legless didn't drink himself to death, but we only half believed him, especially as Úna told us she would never fall in love like her mother had done and end up having babies all the time and sleeping in the same bed as a man smelling of stout who farted.

1968

The school holidays came. We had the long, bright days ahead of us to enjoy, but that summer of 1968 was different. First, Evelyn started wearing high heels. Kait and Úna got jobs like grown-ups do and I helped start the youth club.

Ev was the first of our gang to wear high heels. Before school finished, we went with her to buy the high heels she had seen in the window of Callaghan's shoe shop on Church Street. The shoes were a light, beige-orangey colour that Rory Callaghan kept calling 'salmon coloured.' We found the term 'salmon coloured' hilarious and it put us on the verge of a serious outburst of laughter. Certain things or words got us into fits of giggles. Our bodies quivered and rocked as laughter bubbled up in our bellies like water in a kettle on the hob. We felt it rippling and clasped our mouths shut to keep the giggles gurgling inside, behind our teeth. A glance between us lifted the lid and before we could help it, we were falling about laughing like we had heard or seen the funniest thing ever. At school it always seemed to happen when the Reverend Mother paid a visit. We'd do our best to behave but anything could set us off and we'd feel our bodies trembling with locked-in laughter. If a chuckle escaped out, we'd put our hand in front of our mouth and try to disguise the spurting giggle as a cough.

The day we went with Ev to buy the shoes was one of those giggle-bubbling times. The third time Rory Callaghan called the shoes 'salmon-coloured,' knowing we were about to burst out laughing into his face, the three of us jumped up like lightening from the bench and bolted out the door, leaving Ev alone on the giggly ship.

Afterwards she told us she sucked her cheeks in and make her mouth tight, so the fit of laughter fell back down her throat. It shook her body but at least it didn't gurgle out. Without raising her eyes and stumbling over her sentences, she paid for the shoes and raced to join us around the corner in the chapel grounds. There, we fell about laughing and saying 'salmon coloured' as we held the high heels up in the air. Me, Úna and Kait looked at them with lots of green in our eyes. We hated Ev for being the first of our gang to start wearing heels.

"I'm going to get a job and save my wages up and buy a pair in September," Kait said.

"Me too," Úna said.

"Me three," I said.

"You don't need to save, Ar, ye have plenty of money," Úna and Kait said at the same time, nearly in tones of giving out to me.

"I mightn't need to save but I still have to convince my mother that everyone is wearing high heels."

"Everyone? Evelyn, you mean?" Úna said.

"My mother is so stupid. She says I am too tall as it is without adding more height to me with heels."

"You're nearly normal," Evelyn said looking up at me.

I imitated my mother's voice, "Mary, don't you realise men don't go out with tall girls?" My friends laughed.

"What does Chester Cake Mouth have to say?" Úna wanted to know.

"He makes it worse telling me I should be petit and dainty like my mother."

"Does he want you to cut off half your legs to be smaller?" Ev said.

"Ya, he wants to shove them in his gob along with the Chester cake."

"Don't mind Chester Cake Mouth. Ask your father to buy you the shoes, you're his *peata*," Kait advised.

"I can't because I'd cause a row between the pair of them. Besides, he always does what Mam wants."

"Get a job like me and buy them with your own money," said Úna.

"Where are you going working?" The three of us said looking at her surprised.

"Quinns!"

As soon as she said that, we burst into Manfred Mann's *The Might Quinn*.

"*Come all without, come all within*
You'll not see nothing like the mighty Quinn."

Mr McNulty got Úna the job minding the children in the pub where he drank. Quinn's pub was in High Street, on one of the corners of *An Lár*, near the town hall and across from the drapery shop. It was more than a pub because there were a few businesses on the same premises – a shop, a butcher's, a pub and they did funerals with their hearse. It all belonged to the Quinns.

"Imagine Úna, you'll be the first of us to get a summer job."

"I could get one too," Kait said, "only I have to go for an interview to Sligo and I'm frightened to go on the bus by myself."

"What kind of a job is it?" Ev asked Kait who told us she had answered an ad for a general help in a guest house and a letter came, telling her to come for an interview.

"I never went on the bus by myself. Mam can't come so I don't know if I'll go for the interview."

"A course you have to. I'll come with you," I said.

"I'll go too because I need to buy make-up. So we're all off to Sligo *in the green, in the green, to the echo of a Thomason gun,*" Ev said. Being in love made her burst into song all the time.

"What are you buying more make-up for?"

"Cos in September, Ricky's going to a boarding school in Enniskillen and I betcha those Northern ones are like the English Dolly Bird girls we see on Top of the Pops. I'll make sure he doesn't forget me."

"He won't and now with the high heels, there is no way he'll forget you."

"I'll make sure he won't. I'm going to look fantastic all the time he's still here."

Only three of us went to Sligo on the bus. Úna couldn't come as she was minding the children.

"Don't worry Úna, we'll buy you some grey or brown mascara in that shop over the bridge for ya."

"Thanks a million girls but don't get black mascara for anything in the world."

"We're not stupid, with that pale skin of yours black would make your face like a dalmatian dog with two black spots," Ev said. The teenage magazine we all read had a page with beauty tips, so we had become experts on make-up and spent the journey up to Sligo talking about the different tricks to make our eyes look bigger.

Once we got off the bus, we enquired about where the guest house was and walked out to it. We left Kait inside the gate and walked off showing her our crossed fingers. She was nervous and didn't know if she would get the job.

Me and Ev walked back to town and went to the big Woolworth's shop over the bridge. We headed to the make-up counter. Each drawer in the counter was full of the same type of make-up, eye-line pencils, lip stick, eye shadows, bottles of hair lacquer, narrow metal combs with tight-together teeth that you used to back comb your hair. With the long, thin handle on it you could poke the crown of the tangly hair and lift it higher. In the face power drawer, there was liquid fountain and the caked, solid stuff in a thick tube that you twisted like lipstick. We loved the pan stick and used it to cover black heads and pimples. We were sorry poor Kait couldn't be with us in this wonderland but then Ev said, "If she gets the job, she'll be able to come here every day. Look, this pale pan stick make-up is just what I was looking for to cover my freckles. What colour eye pencil will I get?"

"Black but I don't know what eyeshadow looks good with brown eyes. Look this lipstick is nearly white. Get it and you'll look like the English girls."

Ev left the shop armed with the tools she needed to make sure she was stunning so that Ricky wouldn't forget her. She had lacquer to keep her hair in place, a cream-coloured eye shadow to show up her brown eyes, the eye pencil to blacken the rims, the pale pink lipstick to draw attention to her mouth and the pan stick to plaster over any pimple that dared show its head.

Our next stop was to a shop that sold patterns. She bought piles of patterns so her mother could make skirts and shift dresses. She said she'd buy the material in the drapery shop in Drumbron because she had forgotten to bring her new salmon-coloured shoes with the little high heel, that she called 'kitten highs.' As we waited for Kait at the bus station in Sligo, we looked at the patterns Ev had bought.

"You're going to look fab when you're wearing this dress."

"And the high heels will make me taller."

"You can be sure Ricky won't be able to stop falling in love with you," I told her and added. "I wish I had a pair too."

"Aren't ye going to Cavan?"

"We are."

"Well, start hinting to her father now and a few days before ye go, coax him to buy the shoes."

"Ya, but Mammy will still see them and be cross."

"If you don't wear them until you're in Cavan, your mother won't say anything in front of your aunt."

"Ev, you're right! That's what I'll do." Ev was real cute. Even now in Sligo, she wasn't going to buy the material for her dresses until she saw it was the right colour to go with her shoes.

"Look! Kait is coming." We knew straight away she had the job by the smile on her face. She was half skipping and half walking and her whole body said, 'I'm happy.'

"Tell us, tell us!" we begged as we stood in front of her.

"The woman of the house is called Mrs Jones and she has a sort of an English accent but not fully. The three children have really strong English accents."

"Were they there too?"

"Ya, because I will be living in their house, so they wanted to see me. Even Mrs Jones' sister, Miss May, spoke to me."

"The whole family of the Mighty Quinn's didn't talk to Úna, did they?" Ev asked.

"Sure they know Mr McNulty, Úna's Dad."

"Anyway, I got the job and will be there until the end of August."

"How much are you getting paid."

"Twenty-one shillings," Kait said proudly. "The first week I'm going to send Mammy my whole wages so she can buy shoes for herself, but I'll keep enough to buy a Battenburg cake and a bottle of lemonade for myself. Can you imagine I'll be able to eat the whole cake without having to cut in into thin slices for every one of my brothers and sisters?"

"You greedy pig. When are you starting?"

"The day after tomorrow because Mrs Jones said I'll need to be taught how to do my work."

"What will you be doing?"

"Serving breakfast to the guests, doing the washing up and cleaning the stairs and halls. At about twelve o'clock, I'll start making the bed and cleaning the guests' rooms."

"That's an awful lot."

"It isn't. She'll help me to put the washing machine on every day and to hang out the clothes."

"You'll be dead out," Ev insisted.

"I won't because I'll have a break for dinner and in the evening, I'll do the ironing."

"I never ironed. Mrs McLoughlin does it in our house," I told them.

"Mrs Jones showed me the pressing iron that's long like a narrow table. You put the folded sheets in and bring the top down on the sheets and on the pillowcases. I can sit on a high stool while I'm doing it."

"Úna only has to mind the children. She doesn't even have to bath them."

"I know but I want to earn some money so I can go to the cinema with ye and pay back Mammy the fare for the bus."

Leaving Childhood Behind

"You can do that with your first wages."
"No because for the first week I don't get paid."
"Why not?"
"Because Mrs Jones is training me for the job and besides, I have to pay for the nylon overall that looks like a dress with sleeves."
"That's not fair."
"Maybe but I want the job. So, what did ye buy?"

We showed her and then we rushed to get on the bus. On the way home we told Kait we'd go to her house to help her pack her case and carry it down to the bus station on the day she was leaving.

At home, Mammy was in a temper as usual. At teatime, she started on me saying my hair was a disgrace. She really hated my fringe which I thought was great.

"My hair is fine."
"You'll go blind, and I don't know how you'll see the ball."
"What ball are you talking about?"
"Tennis balls. You have to learn to play tennis."
"I know how to play."
"You know how to mess about. When we go to Cavan to Aunt Hazel's house, I don't want you making a show of yourself."
"I won't."
"I know you won't because John was kind enough to speak to Pat Smith about giving you lessons. He'll be waiting for you tomorrow in the tennis court at one o'clock."

Later when I went to Kait's house to help her pack, Ev was there. She had convinced her mother to buy her another pair of high heels for her birthday.

"Ah Ev, I thought you'd come with me to the tennis court? I don't want to go on my own."

"And Úna and Kait? Can't they go with you?"

"Their mammies don't have money to pay for the lessons."

"Ev, you know Ricky Martin is always mitching school and hanging around Castle Fields," Úna told her.

"I know that well," she said looking at me. "I might be able to go after I get my shoes."

The next morning, Úna and me went with Kait to the station. On the way down the town we saw Nuala, the girl that sat at the desk between ours and helped me decorate the blackboard for the nuns' feast days, so she tagged along too. I was telling Úna and Nuala how I hated going on my own to tennis.

"If I had a racquet, I'd go with you."

"Would you? Tell you what, I'll slope Mammy's one out for you."

"Won't your mother want it?"

"I don't think she knows she has a racquet. Besides since she started playing golf, she's always in the golf course."

After we waved Kait off to Sligo and Úna went to the Quinn's, me and Nuala went to the tennis court. She was as tall as me and with long, nut-coloured hair.

"Nuala, tie your hair in a ponytail. It's handier," I told her as I pulled mine back and gathered it in an elastic band and handed her one too.

She said, "I hate my hair." It was wavy, nearly curly, so I understood why she hated it. We all wanted to be like Sandie Shaw. I was lucky because mine was straight, and I didn't have to iron it on the ironing board like Nuala did.

"I told Alison…"

"Alison?"

"My sister, I told her to iron it, but she cleared off. This stupid hair is so thick," she said as she struggled to get the band on.

"I'll do for you. As least it's long and brown. Poor Úna's is red. She never stops checking to see if it's growing."

"Some girls' hair doesn't grow much. Why is that?"

"Don't know. My mother cuts hers like Jackie Kennedy but she got vexed when I cut mine like Sandie Shaw."

"Does your mother like Jackie?

"She does. When President Kennedy was shot, you'd think it was someone belonged to her who had died."

"Imagine if we had a president young and handsome like him instead of old Dev."

"My mother hates Dev but she loves the Kennedys. Herself and Mr Delaney drove up to Dublin when Jackie came with her two children."

"Why didn't you go?"

"To be stuck in the car with Mr Delaney is too much of a penance."

I was glad me and Nuala were becoming chums. Before she started hanging out with our gang, we used sort of snigger behind her back because the boys called her Drumbron's Rachel Walsh. She had breasts long before the rest of us and looked like a woman. When ours appeared they were small, a size 32 bra or as Ev used to say, when we learned the minus numbers in maths class, a -32. Ev was a little bigger than us with a 34 bra while Nuala must have been a 36.

Boys noticed Nuala so it was no wonder that Pat Smith, the fellow who was in charge of the tennis court, let her in free. He didn't let Úna in when she appeared at the gate of the enclosed area pushing a pushchair with the Quinn kids.

"Pat, let Úna in too. She's only going to look and not play."

"I can't. If the kids get in the way and a ball hits them, I'd be held responsible."

We argued a bit more with Pat but in the end, we gave up because the two the kids started getting cranky and wiggling out of the pushchair.

"I'm taking these two little brats to where there are slides and swings but I'm telling ye, if I had my own pram, there be no fear of them getting out of it." We laughed remembering the big-bellied pram we had pushed all over Drumbron when we were small.

When Ev arrived a while later, it wasn't to play but to take off her flat tennis-shoes and put on her high heels and go off with Ricky Martin, who was waiting for her on the bridge. I didn't care because playing tennis with Nuala was great. She slammed the ball over the net hard at me and I had to run and leap up to be able to hit it back and the few pointers Pat Smith gave us helped us play better.

For the first few days, after practice, we hung around the tennis court chatting about the game. Then I started walking with her as far as the graveyard gate, where we chatted another while before I went in through the cemetery to the railway tracks and took the shortcut back home and she went to her house on Tobair Benin Road. One day she told me to come into her house and we could listen to Joe Dolan and Sandie Shaw on a record-player that her brother Tom had bought in Dublin.

It was like a square case that you opened. Nuala used to stand on the bed and take out the light bulb and plug the cord from the record player into the socket. It was great not having to wait for Jimmy Saville's radio programme to hear our favourite songs. We didn't have many records, so we still listened to Top of the Pops and danced about in her kitchen too.

Her mother was a Protestant who converted when she married Mr McCabe. Mrs McCabe was the same as all the other mothers except Nuala kept to mealtimes with no eating in between. She'd never run into her house for a slice of bread like we did. She even had fixed times to do her lessons.

I was lucky I met Nuala that morning I was going to the station with Kait because I had a new friend. One day in the kitchen I was showing Nuala how to do some set-dancing steps I was learning in Miss Canny's School of Irish Dancing. Our legs were up in the air and as stiff as a boards when her mother came in.

"Ach this kitchen is too small. It's a pity there isn't a place where yis young ones could go to dance," she said as she opened the dresser and took some cups. I thought her accent was a bit like my father's.

"If only," Nuala said.

"The parish hall near the hospital is where the people who want to dance go." I said as I knew my father helped Fr Mannion there.

"What kind of dances do they do?" Mrs McCabe asked.

"Waltzes, foxtrots and quick steps, old people's dances." I answered.

"No thanks," Nuala said making a disgusted face, "I don't want that."

"Girls, I'm just saying if yis could have a place where yis could go dancing, it would be nice."

"I know Mam, but we want to be able to dance like they do on the Top Of The Pops."

"Maybe the older ones would let us use the parish hall. What do you think, Mrs McCabe?" I asked.

"Yis'll have to ask who is in charge of the hall," she said as she set the table and then went out to the press and got out the bread.

"Is it the priest?"

"It is," I answered.

She said simply, "Then ask him." And went out to the back kitchen to get the tea ready.

"How do you know it's the priest's hall?" Nuala asked me.

"My father goes there on Monday nights to play cards with the Men's Club."

"How does that make it the priests?"

"Cos it does. Last Christmas Dad wanted to do a Card Drive and they had to get permission from Fr Mannion. The priest is in charge of everything in Drumbron."

"Then we'll go to him and ask if we can have a Top of the Pops there on Friday nights."

"We'll call it a discotheque. Maybe it's better to get a grown up to talk to Fr Mannion." I suggested.

"Why?"

"He's an awful yoke."

"Alright but what grown up?"

"Miss Kelly?" I said as I didn't know anyone else who was holy and in with the priest.

"Miss Walsh from the library would be better," Nuala's mother said from the back-kitchen.

"Why would she be better?" I asked Nuala's mother in surprise because I never saw Miss Walsh in the chapel like Miss Kelly and the other holy ones.

"Because all the men like her, even the priests."

"I never knew that."

"It's true. She's the one to talk to Fr Mannion, but Arlene, get your father to soften her up for yis." Mrs McCabe said.

"Why?"

"He is a great friend of hers. Nuala's dad said when there's a card game, Miss Walsh is your father's partner at the table."

"A course," I said pretending I knew they were friends.

The evening at home I asked Daddy how we could start a youth club in the parish hall.

"What kind of club would that be?"

"Where we can dance."

"To a showband."

"No, Daddy, you silly goose. We just want to listen to records of the Beatles and Brendan Boyer, like the girls on the TV."

"You got the hair already, so I understand you want to shake it about." Daddy knew my hair was causing trouble between Mammy and me. She thought it was a disgrace I wore it long with a split in the middle and let it hang down on my two shoulders. She used to say I'd wake up one morning and I would find it cut off me. In my dreams I saw her creeping into room with scissors in her hands, so I tucked it inside the back of my nightdress. I woke up every morning relieved I still had my hair but knowing once I went downstairs, she would attack it with all her verbal might.

"Mary, come here, I'm going to plait your hair for you. You can't go to school with it hanging down like that."

"It's fine."

"No, it isn't."

I'd grab a piece of toast and hurry out of the kitchen. She'd come after me with a brush and a ribbon as though I were small. "I'm not pulling my hair back. There no Home Babies in the class so I won't get lice or nits." I'd shout a retort like that at her and run out the front door banging it with all my might.

She'd call after me, "Get that hair out of your eyes or when you get up tomorrow morning there won't be a rib on your head."

Daddy knew about our hair rows so that is why he mentioned my swinging hair.

"Where will your hair be dancing?"

"The parish hall."

"And when?"

"Friday nights."

"Who'll go?"

"Us, me and my friends."

"Dance here in the house."

I glanced at Mammy's magazine but didn't say 'with that wan around trying to plait the girls' hair' and just said, "There'll be plenty of us and there's no room here for the girls from the Mercy and the boys from the Brothers."

"A real youth club then?"

"A course Daddy, we aren't babies. We need a place where we can meet. Nuala said we'd put posters up, so we'd get a good crowd."

"Can I come too?"

"No, it's only for us from secondary school. That why we`re calling it the youth club. Nuala and I thought we'd get Miss Kelly to talk to the priest because she's in charge of the Legion."

"Not a good idea. She'd have you praying instead of dancing.

I'll talk to Fr Mannion and yis talk to Imelda in the library about the posters."

"Imelda?"

"Miss Walsh, she is very efficient and will help you. When yis talk to Fr Mannion tell him a committee is in charge of things."

"A committee!"

"Yes. Give my name and Imelda Walsh's name, and say we are members of the committee."

The Youth Club

The whole summer was taken up with getting the club started. There was an awful lot of walking from here to there, talking to this person and that, like Miss Walsh, who got us a meeting with Fr Mannion.

"Father we were wondering if you might be able to help us?" I asked half stuttering, knowing he'd go back and tell Mr Delaney.

"In what way?" he asked in his gruff voice, half turned away from us.

"Well, you know lots of boys and girls from Drumbron go to Sligo because there is a youth club there," Nuala said in a firm voice that made the priest turn around fully and stare at her.

"I do and what has that to do with you, Miss McCabe?"

"We thought if we started a youth club in the parish hall no one would have to go to Sligo."

"Isn't that very thoughtful of you, young lady," he said with a mocking tone.

But Nuala didn't lower her eyes and answered, "I'm only saying it would be a good idea to have a youth club in our own town."

"A big undertaking for one so young, surely."

"Maybe but I'm not on my own, there is a committee to run it."

"A committee! And who's on this committee that I know nothing about?"

"My father knows all the names," I stuttered again.

"Your father?"

"Miss Walsh from the Library and Garda Curry are on it, too."

"And Mrs Rose McCabe," Nuala added, giving her mother's name.

"Let me think about this and I'll inform your father of my decision," he said and walked away making a sound similar to 'pushing against heavy material' the nuns used to make with their long habits. We waited for what seemed ages, but it was only a week before Fr Mannion gave Daddy the go-ahead and a set of keys for the parish hall. Me and Nuala went with him to see the place where we going to have our youth club.

The wide wooden door opened in the middle and we went in behind Daddy and gazed in wonder at this dream come true, where we could dance to the songs we heard on Radio Luxemburg. The hall was a long, wide rectangle shape with the stage at the far end from the door. Awed, we hurried along the long, dusty wooden boards of the floor.

"Yis lasses will have to sweep the floor and put talcum powder on it so yis can dance."

"Do we, is that what you do?"

"Aye, Imelda comes in the morning, and we sweep and get the floor ready for dancing." I didn't know Daddy went dancing but at the moment I was too gobsmacked to care. Only a week ago we were wishing we could have a place to get together and now we were actually in the place where it was going to happen. Me and Nuala walked close to together, our hips bumping, looking at each other every now and then to make sure this was real as we surveyed the place that would make our dreams come true.

The bottom part of the wall was painted brown, shiny with little grains like crepe paper that was topped off by a thick, bulging-out band of beige that Mammy would have called a border if it were wallpaper like we had in our sitting room. From the border up it was white – gone a darker shade of dirtier, dusty yellowish-beige to the ceiling. Chairs were stacked up in lots of seven in front of the stage.

"Dad, why are the chairs there?" I called my father Dad when my friends were around, otherwise they would think I was a baby if I called him Daddy.

"For the people to sit on when they are not dancing. Yis lasses can line them along the walls. Imelda will be only too happy to help yis."

"That's very kind of you, Superintendent Blake." The polite, agreeable tone Nuala was using when she spoke to my father was the complete opposite to the one she used with Fr Mannion. "Who knows, we might manage on our own, but if we don't, we'll be delighted to ask Miss Walsh to help us."

The stage had steps on the right-hand side. We were heading towards them when Daddy said, "Let's see where the toilets are." He led us to the left side of the stage. There was a door with *Mná* written on it. Inside there was a handbasin and two doors with toilets behind them. Down a bit there was another door with *Fir* on it, but we didn't want to go in.

"Superintendent Blake, do you mind if we go up on the stage? You see we might need to plug in the record player in the light socket if we don't find a socket on the wall."

"No problem, but first place two chairs in front of the stage because I want yis wee lasses to watch my magic show," Daddy said going up the few steps that lead to the stage. On stage, my father stood beside a chair with a headscarf covering it, pretending he had a magic wand in his hand, acting like he was Paul Daniels, the magician on TV. I was a bit ashamed and was going to say, 'Stop acting the eejit, Daddy.' when he caught the scarf by two corners and swiped it off. A record-player was sitting on the chair. Me and Nuala started screaming our heads off. Daddy picked up the cord and said "Abracadabra!" and shook his fingers at it saying, "I command you to grow."

It got longer and longer as he unwound it, making it long enough to plug into the socket on the wall. We wouldn't have to stand on the chair and unscrew the bulb to be able to plug it in. We were jumping up and down and hugging each other when Daddy said, "Careful, Missy, that hair of yours is flying all over the place."

I didn't like him calling me Missy in front of Nuala, but I was so happy that I forgave him. I turned to thank him when I saw he was holding a record in his hand. We stood still, barely able to breathe when we saw it was *Puppet on a String* by Sandie Shaw. Daddy put it on the player and me and Nuala came to life again and started dancing, throwing our arms up in the air like the girls did on Top of The Pops.

"It's up to yis lasses to get the hall ready and have things in place for the opening night."

"What things, Dad?"

"Well before the dance…"

"It's not a dance Dad, it's a discotheque."

"Fine, but you will need to be here before the public arrives."

"The public?"

"Your friends who come to dance. The floor is always a mess, so yis will need to sweep it before yis take the chairs down and place them against the walls."

"Why do we need chairs? We're going to dance!"

"So ye will have somewhere to sit when you're not dancing."

"I suppose."

"Then someone needs to check there is toilet paper in the toilets."

"I never thought of that, but you are right, Superintendent Blake," Nuala said in her nicely toned voice.

"And the music, we'll have to change the record every now and then too, I suppose," I said.

"Aye, the record will need to be changed but the player can be left here no bother."

"Are you sure no one will take it, Superintendent Blake?" Nuala asked in her sweet tone.

"They won't because do yis see this key here?" Daddy said showing us a yale lock type key.

"Ya, what's it for, Dad?"

"For the press under the stage. You can keep the record player locked in there."

"That's a great idea, Superintendent Blake."

I was getting a tiny bit annoyed with Nuala plasmásing my father so much. I said, "I want to take the new record home, I don't want to leave it here."

"That's fine but lasses it's always better to have one or two here in case yis forget to bring some on the night." I saw that made sense and I was realising Daddy was very clever and knew plenty of things. Maybe that's why Nuala looked at him as though he was great.

"Daddy, can I play my accordion?"

"Will yis young ones want to listen to that kind of music?"

"Superintendent Blake, when Arlene plays *The Boys Won't*

leave The Girls Alone it's great craic and we all want to jump around the place."

"Well if that's the story, go ahead. Yis know what the young ones like better than me. Fr Mannion will want the National Anthem played at the end of the night. It's the custom."

"Úna's brother Declan plays the tin whistle. We can get him to do the National Anthem cos it was one of the first things he learned with Danny Kelly."

"Declan who?"

"Declan McNulty from Dun na Rí. He goes to the Brothers."

"A McNulty! That would be his father's doing alright, getting his son to learn *Amhrán na bhFiann*."

That was one of the few times I ever heard Daddy talk Irish. His accent was a bit funny, so I said, "Dad, how do you say *a grá*?"

He said '*A graaa*' with a real high A.

We tried not to laugh cos it sounds so different from the way we said it, I suppose it was a bit like the way he spoke in English.

"Daddy, me and Nuala are going to do the poster this week."

"Why are yis doing that so soon?"

"Cos we're going to Cavan soon and I mightn't have time when we get back."

"Good, Imelda thinks like yis. The notices need to be up as soon as possible, so the word spreads and plenty of yis turn up on the first night."

"When exactly are we going to Cavan, Dad? Is it at the end of August?"

"The week after next. Yis have next week to do all that

is needed to be done, Arlene, and yis can give the posters to Imelda. She'll find young ones to hang them up."

"That's great, Superintendent, because I am going to the Gaeltacht the second last week of August," Nuala said looking at my father as though he was a fine yoke.

"So, you are off learning Irish, are you?"

"Yes, my mother loves the Irish Language."

"Isn't your mother one of the Armstrong's from Leitrim?"

"She is," Nuala said, seeming pleased my father knew about her family.

"And she speaks the Irish herself?"

"She does. My grandmother was a distant cousin of Douglas Hyde."

"The first President of Ireland."

"And the founder of the Gaelic League. Mammy is very proud of him and saved all year so we can go and learn Irish," Nuala gushed looking at my father as though wanting his approval.

"I know your father well. Tom McCabe, he works in the Meat Factory, isn't that right?"

So much talk between the two of them was getting on my nerves so I said, "Dad stop talking and tell us where the brushes are. We have a lot to do and have no time for talking."

"My bossy wee lass."

Getting the Hall Ready

We spent the week cleaning the hall and getting it ready. Daddy gave me money to buy whatever we needed, like crepe paper which we used to make lovely decorations of colourful chains that we were going to drape around the walls on the first night. We painted 'Drumbron Youth Club 13th September 1967' in fancy letters on an old white sheet Mrs McLoughlin had been going to cut up for dusters. She gave it to me when I told what I wanted it for. The sheet looked like an enormous poster. Daddy said he would nail it on top of the stage on the opening night.

So while Kait was in Sligo in the guesthouse, Úna was with the Quinns and Ev was chasing Ricky, I spent all my time with Nuala. When I told her I was going to Cavan to see my cousin Sammy she said, "Is your cousin really called Sammy?"

I knew there was no Sammy in Drumbron, so I thought she might be laughing at the name. I answered in a huff and tried to imitate Dad's Garda voice. "He is because he's from Cavan."

"I must tell Mammy. She will be delighted because my granddaddy is Samuel." Once I knew that, I relaxed and told her how nice Sammy was and how he looked like my father.

"Does he ever come here?"

"Not really."

"What a pity. Mammy would love to meet another Samuel."

"I'll try and convince him to come to see our youth club. Can you imagine, Nuala, we will have the first Discotheque of the Drumbron youth club when we come back!"

"Ya, on Friday the thirteenth."

"It will bring us good luck so don't be worrying about it."

She smiled and answered, "Not a notion of me worrying. *Go n eiri an bóthar leat.* Safe journey." We hugged and left the parish hall. I was floating on air until I got home where I found Mammy annoyed that I hadn't gone to the hairdressers.

"Where were you, Mary? I told Peggy you'd have your hair washed and set."

"I couldn't go because me and Nuala were tidying the youth club."

"No need to tell me. Look at the cut of you, like one of those hippies in America. What kind of an impression you are going to make on Aunt Hazel, I don't know!"

Chester Cake Mouth had the cheek to say, "Dervla, she'll never have your style, so even if she went to the Peggy's, she'd still have that wild hair."

"Better than being half bald like you," I said because Mr Delaney combed a few wisps of hair across his head trying to pretend he had hair.

"Mary, how dare you talk to John like you did. If you don't behave, we'll see if you go to the discotheque, and I'll put a stop to you wearing your skirt above your knees. You're getting way out of hand for my liking."

"A firm hand is what is needed. The country is going to the devil with marches and protests all over the place."

"Who would ever have thought we'd have the farmers holding the country to a standstill. It would be more in the line of The National Farmers' Association to get the county men to plough their fields instead of protesting."

"And the ones in the North copying the blacks in America. No wonder the RUC and the police had to baton-charge them to put manners on them."

"What were they marching for, John, would you know?"

"They don't even know themselves. I mean throwing stones is something youngsters do, but flour and eggs is another story altogether. The streets must be a right mess with their going on."

I knew he was talking about the students throwing flour and eggs at Terence O'Neill because at Easter, the 1916 Parade was banned. Mr McNulty had said, "What is good for the goose is good for gander. If they ban the commemorations for the fiftieth anniversary of The Rising, let them ban the 12th of July too."

Knowing this, I shouted at Mr Delaney and Mammy, "They want Civil Rights and to be able to vote."

Mammy's eyes nearly popped out of her head.

"Mary, let that be the last time you speak to John like that. Your father is going to hear about this."

"I don't care. If you read the paper, you'd know a young, single, Unionist woman was given a house and there was plenty of women with big families on the list waiting for that house long before her."

"Really Mary, with all the magazines I have to look at and you want me to read the papers," she answered as though it was normal that she hadn't a clue what was happening in her own country.

I opened my mouth to tell her so when Mouth spoke down to me as though I were stupid like my mother. "Let me explain that to you, Mary."

"What's to explain? That it is unfair to leave people for years without a house," I said in my Garda voice.

"Mary, what you don't know is that those people broke the law when they occupied the premises."

"They didn't."

"They did. They occupied the house without permission from the authorities. The police had to remove them as they were breaking the law," he continued saying in a patronising tone.

"Breaking a law that is unjust. I'd do the same."

Mammy gasped and Mr Delaney went to her. "Are you alright, Dervla?"

I ran upstairs to my room and banged the door shut. I knew what was happening in the North because Mr McNulty told us about the Civil Rights Student Movement and how the young people were asking for the same rights as the Unionists had. He said things were going to change big-time in Ireland and it was about time.

Sometimes I felt like Janus, the ancient Roman God with his two faces, only it was two minds I had. One of them was filled with what Mammy and Mouth said and the other with what Mr McNulty said. I heard two sharply contrasting opinions about everything. Thank God Dad had no opinion on anything, so I could smile and be his bonny wee lass.

While me and Nuala were in the parish hall preparing things for the youth club, Dad called in everyday to see if we needed anything. It was great having him for myself away from Mammy. I told him about Ev getting high heels. I said all my friend's mothers were buying shoes for their daughters, but Mammy didn't want to get me a pair.

"Arlene, remember how we used not tell Mammy everything so as not to upset her? Well, we'll do the same with the high heels you want."

"What will we do, Daddy?" I asked in a voice like when I was small.

"We'll go to Callaghan's the day before we go to Hazel's and buy the shoes. We won't say a word to Mammy and if you put them at the bottom of your case, she won't know you have them until you wear them in Cavan."

"Daddy, you are clever cos you know Mammy won't cause a scene in Aunt Hazel's." I gave him the biggest squeeze I could and told him he was the best daddy in all Ireland, England and broad Scotland and we went to Cavan with the shoes at the bottom of my case.

Aunt Hazel was standing at the door as we drove up the driveway. She shook Mammy's hand but hugged and kissed me. She then held me back to look at me as though she couldn't believe what she was seeing. "You're so beautiful, your mother's looks and colouring and our height. Bill, what a delightful daughter you have, you must be so proud." Daddy nodded, a big smile on his face.

Sammy had changed. He was taller and had a wider body the whole way down. Michael Stiff-Neck had wide shoulders but slimmer hips with long legs. Sammy was tall and broad but with the bottom part of his body wider than the lads in Drumbron. His pinkish-white face was broader too, not hatchet-shaped or russet like most of the lads at home. Even his eyes were a light blue, like Daddy or Liam's, not the cloudy blue of Ricky and Jim Smith's. I was looking at him and taking him in as a boy, not as a cousin, because Nuala had asked me a lot of questions about him. When I went back, I wanted to be able to describe him.

The week went really fast. The first few days we went *a chéile*-ing to Daddy's family houses. In Drumbron '*a chéile*' meant dancing, while in Cavan it was a get together. We'd go for a chat, stay for tea and wouldn't leave until late in the evening.

Me, Sammy and Daddy went climbing the Cuilleach Mountains. Daddy parked the car in a place called Achadh na Coille, The Wood Fields and we climbed to the top and looked at the wondrous world below us.

Another day we left Ballyconell and drove through a twisty trail that wound along cliff sides and gaps and steep falls and sheep grazing on the patches of green ground among the rocky grey surface. After feeling I was with the poet Coleridge coming down from Lebanon 'through mountain bleak and brown' we arrived in Dowra. From there, the road was normal, and we got to Ballinaglera, which was a few houses at the bottom of a mountain. The road sign pointing up towards a mountain said *Sliabh an Iarainn*, but Dad and Sammy were calling it *The Iron Mountain*.

Daddy stopped the car outside a pub, and we went in. It was like a kitchen with two counters. Near the door was the first counter, the shop one, with a wooden dresser behind it. The shelves were stacked with tins of peas and beans and peaches as well as packets of tea and sugar. There was a sack of flour on the ground near the dresser and another of potatoes.

Across from the door a fireplace was warming three old men sitting on chairs in front of it. There was a dog lying beside one of the chairs. The other counter had a woman behind it. She was pulling a pint for the customer who was standing at the bar. Dad went to that counter and got an orange-ade and a packet of Tayto for me and Sam and a pint of stout for himself. They wanted to know who we were. Dad knew how to reply without telling them what they asked.

On Sunday, our last day, we went to a service for my Daddy's grandfather who had died during the war. It was in a small town. Mammy had a bit of a headache and didn't come. Afterwards while we were having dinner, I told her there was no red light in front of the Tabernacle and that the priest was standing on a podium reading from a lectern that was shaped like an eagle.

"Mammy, I didn't go up to Communion because Daddy told me not to go."

"It doesn't matter, you can go next Sunday."

"The priest looked at me awful funny at the end of the Mass."

"Were you misbehaving?"

"Of course I wasn't but I think it was because I was the only one who blessed myself."

Aunt Hazel looked at Dad and said laughing, "Bill, we all know it's hard to get you inside a church, but doesn't Arlene know you are not a Roman Catholic?"

"Hazel, I never had time for religion, so it's not something I have long conversations about with my daughter," Daddy said in his Garda voice.

Later when me and him and Mammy were in the garden, I said to him, "Daddy, I know you are not a Catholic."

"He's not a Catholic or anything else. If he believed in any religion, I would have had him converted long ago," Mammy said.

"Daddy, you can't be nothing."

"I was born in the Anglican faith but as your mother says, I have no time for any of the organised religions."

"But we went to the mass today."

"In honour and respect for my grandfather who lost his life fighting for his Queen and country."

Great-granddaddy Blake

"For the Queen? Was my great-granddaddy Blake English?"

"He was born in here in Cavan but at a time when we were still part of the British Empire."

"I know about that. Last year in history we did the Rising of 1916."

"Granddad didn't have much time for that. He considered the ones who fought as traitors of the Empire."

"But they were heroes."

"For some. My grandfather had other ideas. He was proud to be one of the thousands who signed the Ulster Covenant."

I didn't know what the Ulster Covenant was, so I thought I'd ask Mr McNulty to hear what he had to say. He was like Dad; he didn't go to Mass either.

"What was your daddy's name?"

"William."

"Nuala's grandfather's name is Samuel. Me and her are the same, only her father is the Catholic and her mother the Protestant."

"Is Nuala McCabe's mother a Protestant?" Mammy asked surprised.

"She isn't now because she converted to marry Nuala's father. Did you convert too Dad?"

"He didn't." Mammy's tone implied he had committed a crime.

"You didn't, Daddy.

"That is why we were married in the side church, hidden

away from everyone." Mammy's eyes were as hard as blue marbles, and her lips were just lines around her teeth.

"Mammy, you didn't walk down the aisle like Úna's, I mean Evelyn's mother?"

"I didn't, but you will. We'll make up for the wedding I didn't have, by making yours the best wedding Drumbron has ever seen," she said with such certainty that I had to put her straight.

"But Mammy, I have no boyfriend," I said looking in my head for a boy I really liked. The images of the lads that popped up were pushed out of my mind real quick, except that of Michael Stiff Neck.

"Here's comes Sammy," Daddy said pointing to my cousin who was waving tennis rackets and dangling keys. "I'd say he wants to drive you to the tennis court for a game." When I got in the car and we were on the road, I told Sammy about the youth club me and Nuala were starting.

"Nuala? So your friend is called Fionnuala like the daughter in The Children of Lír?"

"She's got a long neck, but her hair is brown, so I don't think she's like Aoife."

"Is she on Lough Derravara?" he asked, showing off so I would know he had read the story.

"She's not. She is in the Gaeltacht." Names are funny. Nuala wanted to know about Sammy because of his name. Now he wanted to know about Nuala because of her name.

On Saturday the 6th of September, as we were leaving Cavan, my cousin whispered to me he would drive down to Drumbron the following Friday if I promised to introduce him to my friend, Nuala of the swan's neck.

We Meet At Mass

Kait had arrived back Friday evening, a day before me. Ev was busy on Saturday saying goodbye to Ricky, so the four of us didn't meet up until Sunday at the side door of the church. We wanted to scream and jump and hug each other but we behaved like young ladies as people were going into Mass.

Of the four of us, Úna was the one of us who had changed the most. She was more filled out with no hollow spaces under her cheek bones. Her lips looked plump and juicy with the lip gloss. Instead of the thick, white eyelashes that we always saw on her, she had brown fringes covering her blue eyes and no glasses. She actually looked beautiful.

We were all wearing our new heels and about to look down at them when we saw Mary O'Rourke make a sign with her hand that we were come and sit in our places in the Sodality pew, which we did. Going up to Communion, one behind the other in a line, and listening to the clicky-clacky sound was lovely.

After Mass we dallied around, stopping and talking to all the girls we knew so they could see we were wearing high heels and then we hurried over to the bridge in Castle Fields to tell each other our news.

Looking at Kait's lips, Ev said, "You look great, is that 'The Palest of Pink' you are wearing?"

"Do you like it? I was going to save all my money, but then thought, sugar it, I'll buy a few things for myself. I bought these high heels too, so I could wear them this Sunday. I love yours

Úna, and yours Arlene. Now I wish I had got a light colour and not this brown."

"Brown goes with everything. It's the best colour really," I said even though I really thought my fawn ones were nicer.

"Kait, your mother told me about you sending her the money in an envelope without an address," Úna said laughing, so we wanted to know what had happened.

"Ah, I was stupid! When I got my first week's money, I was so excited I asked Mrs Jones for an envelope and a stamp. While she was getting it from a desk in the hall, I scribbled a quick note to Mammy, telling her to buy a pair of shoes for herself with the pound note inside. I shoved the note and pound inside the envelope and rushed out to the green pillar post-box in front of the guest house. It was only when I had pushed it through the slit, I realised I hadn't written the address on it."

"Oh my God, your first wages down the drain," Ev said.

"What did you do?" I asked.

"I started crying and ran back to the house and told Mrs Jones."

"And?"

"She said that I had to write a letter to the General Post Office in Dublin explaining what had happened."

"And?"

"A week later I got the envelope back inside a big envelope, but my letter was opened. I was so ashamed."

"Why?"

"Because everyone would have read my letter telling my mother I wanted her to buy herself a pair of shoes with my first wages."

"Why did you want her to buy shoes?" I asked.

"Because she always bought shoes for all of us and never for herself," Kait answered me with a surprised look on her face as though I should have known that.

"Aw, sure the ones in Dublin wouldn't know you, so it's no harm. They can't be talking behind yer backs about ye having no money for shoes," Úna said, fully understanding the reason for Kait's shame.

"What was it like with the Mighty Quinn?"

That question was all we needed to start singing, "*Come all without, come all within. You ain't seen nuthing like the Might Quinn.*"

Which didn't bother Úna and she told us, "It was great, they are as nice as can be. The nights I was babysitting I could eat all the food I wanted."

"Naturally. That is normal," I said.

"For you it might be but the food in our house goes real quick."

"In my house too," Kait said.

"Anyway, it was great. I used to stuff myself with brown bread and butter. Once I ate nearly the whole cake that Mrs McKenna had made that day."

"Who's Mrs McKenna?"

"The woman who comes in to mind the house."

"I love the brown bread that Mrs McLoughlin makes in our house."

"Did you sleep in their house?" Ev asked.

"No, Mr Quinn drove me home."

"Mr Quinn is lovely. He's a friend of Dr Kelly, they play cards together." I let them know I knew Daddy went to the card games with them.

"I know he is but his friend, that Howlin man, is horrible," Úna told us.

"I heard stories about him," Kait added.

"What do you mean?" Ev asked.

"He's supposed to have got a lot of girls into trouble."

"No way," I said.

"Well, it could be because he drove me down by Castle Fields to talk to me."

"He didn't."

"He did, I told him I wanted to go home but he said it was nice and quiet and we could talk in peace."

"What did he want to talk about?"

"He asked me if ever I had been kissed."

"What's it to him, the dirty old man!" Ev said, offended he had the nerve to ask Úna that.

"That's exactly what I told him. I said my father wouldn't like an old man like him to be asking me questions like that."

"You said that?" I asked, surprised Úna could have been so cheeky.

"It's true. His youngest daughter is about ten. Himself and Mr Quinn are well older than our fathers, so they are," Kait informed us.

"He's like Mouth Delaney, as old as the hills," I added because he was ancient.

"And what did he say to that, Úna?" Ev asked.

"He got annoyed and said it was most likely no boy ever kissed me because I'm ugly."

"That's not true, what a pig to say that. You look great with the mascara on," I said in case she believed the stupid man.

"He can say what he wants but I wouldn't kiss him for all

the tea in China. I know the ones to keep away from because Mammy warned me about them."

"Who are they?" I wanted to know while Ev was saying, "Tell us."

"You be surprised. There's even a few in the Vincent de Paul who have got an awful name," Kait said shocking us.

"I heard Mammy talking about them ones too. To get the 2/6 from the Vincents, the women have to be nice to the men when they call into the house." Seeing how our faces had changed and the disgust on them, Úna volunteered some information we had never heard before. "Some of the serving girls Mr Howling's mother had working for her ended up in the Home," she told us.

"You mean the serving girls had Home Babies?"

"I think that is what Mammy meant."

"You were lucky, Úna, he didn't make you have a baby too," I said.

Ev asked, "Did he drive you home at least?"

"He did because I said my father would be annoyed and might get his gun out if he let me walk home at night from Castle Fields." The McNultys were known as Republicans, so Úna was right to have frightened that stupid fool who got girls put into the Home.

"Kait, did you have any problems like that in Sligo?"

"No, cos Mrs Jones is a widow."

"A widow?"

"Ya, her husband was a Polish doctor. She told me he died and that is why she came back to Sligo to her family, the O'Brien's."

"Is that why the children have English accents?"

"Yes, they are half-English and half-Polish, but Jones is not the right name. Mrs Jones said the Polish surname was difficult to pronounce so they changed it to Jones."

"Why didn't they change it to O'Brien?"

"They want to be English. The children used to laugh at my accent saying I didn't know how to pronounce 'three'."

"They must be stupid or that," Ev said.

I was thinking of Mammy and how she had changed her way of talking so I added, "Or like Prissy-mouth Gay Byrne."

"No, they were nice, just the mother was always talking about how well-mannered the English are. She said I never said please or thank you, but I told her I always say, "That was lovely." when I finished my meal."

"We all say that. It better than thank you because as least you let your mother know you enjoyed the food."

"Mrs Jones thought I hadn't a clue about anything."

"Why would she think that?"

"Cause the first day I had to set the table for breakfast, I didn't know what side the knife or the fork went, so I asked her. She tutted and went on as though it was the worst crime in the world. Once she showed me, I was fine."

"Where do they go?" Úna asked, very interested.

"The knife is for the hand that you bless yourself with, the fork on the other side and the big spoon in front of the soup plate for the corn flakes or the porridge."

"And the small spoon on the saucer."

"Naturally. It didn't take me long to learn everything."

"Did you see anyone you fancied?"

"No, but I saw Jim Smith."

"That's great, did ye have a chat?"

"It wasn't great because he was with that Noeleen wan and a few from Loretta's crowd."

"He wasn't! When was that?"

"One evening I went with the children to see *Chitty, Chitty Bang*."

"Did he talk to you?"

"He didn't see me because we were sitting behind them. Thank God the lights went out quick and no one saw me crying, except Krystiana the youngest of the kids."

"You poor thing."

"I had to lie to Krystiana telling her I had a toothache and that why I was crying."

"Did he see you after?"

"No because he was too busy talking to them all and laughing but that brother of Loretta's, Kevin, saw me."

"Forget about him," I told her and Úna nodded her head in agreement.

"I can't. I keep thinking about Jim all the time," Kait said.

"I'll ask Ricky what's going on."

"Will you? That's good of you, Ev."

"I bet cha it's nothing. Maybe he only went with that crowd cause you weren't around town," I said.

She replied with hope in her voice. "That's it. Tomorrow when we go to the Legion, they'll be waiting for us on the bridge like always."

"Ricky won't be there because he's leaving for the boarding school his father is sending him to," Ev informed us mournfully.

"Poor Ev, you must be heartbroken too."

"I'm trying not to be because Ricky promised he'd write to me every week and when we leave school, we'll get engaged."

"Engaged!" We all screamed as we ran around her jumping up and down not believing what we were hearing, even Kait's face cheered up. It was unbelievable that one of our gang was doing such a grown-up thing as getting engaged.

"That means we'll be bridesmaids!" I shouted because who else would she have, except us?

"What colour will the bridesmaids' dresses be," Kait asked.

"I don't know, first I have to think about the ring. But remember what I'm telling ye is like the third secret of Fatima. No one is to know until me and Ricky tell our parents."

"Kiss my heart and swear to die." We all said as we kissed our fingers and crossed them on our mouths and chests.

"Let's all go to Shatter's jewellery shop tomorrow and look at the rings in the window," Ev said and asked me about what was happening in town.

"Arlene, how were things about town?"

"The same as always. Legless McHugh causing trouble and Chester Cake Mouth is stuck in my house all the time. I went to a few football matches with Dad, and he helped me and Nuala with the youth club."

"A youth club!" Kait screeched.

Ev asked, "Is that true?"

"It is."

"When is it starting?"

"Nuala is coming back from the Gaeltacht tonight, so we are leaving the opening until next Friday the thirteenth."

"Friday thirteenth, the English think it's an unlucky day," Ev said.

"Nanny or Nan never told us it was bad luck, so it isn't for us, only for the English," Úna said.

"They only told us it was bad luck to go in through the front-door and out through the back one, as you took the good luck out of the house," Kait added.

"And they said never to walk inside a fairy ring," I said and as it was Kait's turn again she said, "And to say, 'Mind yerselves when you're throwing out the dishwater!' in the evening in case you wet the fairies."

"Shut up will ye and let us hear about the youth club and not about old women's tales!" Ev screamed at us and looked pointedly at me, ordering me to continue.

"We have the posters ready. Some are up in the library already."

"Ya, I saw one behind Miss Walsh's desk," Ev said, "but I didn't much notice what was on it."

"Well, tomorrow we are going to the three schools to put some on the notice boards, if ye want to help." The three nodded their heads.

"As we don't have too many records, we were asking around for some to play on our new record-player. Úna, your brother Declan, is going to play the National Anthem on his flute."

"And you'll play your accordion?"

"Maybe but the best news is that my cousin Sammy is coming from Cavan."

"We could fix him up with you, Úna?" Ev said.

"We'll see, he lives in Cavan so it's no good having a boyfriend miles away," I said and then realised Ev looked a bit sad as it dawned on her Ricky would be in Enniskillen and miss the opening of the youth club. We headed home for dinner.

That afternoon Ev didn't come with us on the paper round or go to the cinema. As Úna and Kait had some money saved from their summer job, we didn't bother taking the sixpence from the newspaper money to buy a choc-ice or slip into the cinema. The paper round wasn't fun anymore and we started talking about leaving the Legion.

"But we have to go on Tuesday. We can't just leave like that, or Miss Kelly will want to know why," Kait said.

"Alright but we'll find a reason to stop going," I said, and they agreed we'd go for a few more meetings.

Lapsed Catholics

At the next Legion meeting there was a tall, dark-haired, pale-skinned lady wearing a hazel tweed coat with a shiny butterfly broch on the lapel, a beige, crocheted hat, a knitted fawn scarf. Gloves the same tone were lying next to a brown serious-type bag at the top of the table. Miss Kelly introduced the fawny-brown woman as Miss Price-Hyde and Miss Kelly informed us she was the woman in charge of the trips the Legion Members made each summer to England. The woman in question produced a notebook from her handbag. We followed her every movement, hypnotised by what she was doing until we heard Miss Kelly cough. Everyone turned their glace back to her. She said Miss Price-Hyde was interested in getting the names of those interested in going to England and speaking to the Laps.

The golden-yellowy wings of the butterfly on the lapel had me mesmerised, so without thinking I said, "Why are ye going to England, don't the Laps live in Lapland?"

There were titters of laughter and Miss Kelly, looked directly at me and speaking slowly, explained that 'laps' were lapsed Catholics. Members of the Legion went every summer to speak to them and try to bring them back to the church. Evelyn, Kait and Úna were trying not to laugh but everyone knew they were laughing because the held-in giggles were making their bodies shake. Nuala, on the other side with her two friends from her road, pretended she didn't know me.

Miss Kelly gave me another withering look and continued saying it was an important mission, so each September some ladies volunteered. During the year money was collected by raffles and other fundraising activities. Looking at the tall woman dressed in brown and beige she said, "Miss Price-Hyde leads the group every year and I would like to take this opportunity to thank her for her great dedication and hard work and the cheer she brings to this worthwhile initiative. Without doubt, it could be described as going on the missions, saving souls for the church."

Everyone looked at Miss Price-Hyde. She smiled and nodded her thanks for the acknowledgment. Then she stood up and told us she had another engagement she needed to attend. Evelyn touched my leg with her foot. I turned my head into her face. She mouthed, "The Bishop's housekeeper" so I would know the reason why Miss Kelly was playing up to Miss Price-Hyde so much. As the bishop's housekeeper was opening the door to leave, Miss Kelly asked us if we still wanted the same paper route. Kait excused herself and the rest of us by saying we couldn't do the paper round anymore as we had to study for our Inter Cert.

Miss Price-Hyde was at the door but turned around when she heard Kait. She looked at her and said, "You live on Kilmartin Road, don't you?" uttering 'Kilmartin' with a lifting of one side of her lips and then a twisting of her cheek as though she had something with a horrible, disgusting taste in her mouth.

"I do, so I do," Kait replied looking the rigid woman straight in the eye.

"Well, I have this letter here I want you to deliver to Mrs Devine who lives at Number 27," she said as she glanced at the envelope to see the number. "It will save me having to go to that place," she said with the tone of wanting to spit it out of her mouth. Miss Kelly had hopped up and leaped across the room to take the letter from her hand.

"Delia and Maggie go to bed early, so I can't go knocking on their door this late," Kait counter-attacked, not liking one bit the tone the wan was using when referring the road she lived on.

"Naturally, but I want it delivered tomorrow, young lady. The Bishop's express desires were that Mrs Devine received the letter as soon as possible," she said as she stepped out the door and closed it leaving Kait with no chance to reply.

We had been dying for the meeting to finish to see if Jim Smith was on the bridge in Castle Fields. Now we wanted it to finish to ask Kait who this Mrs Devine was and why the bishop was sending her letters.

Jim wasn't on the bridge, but Kait wasn't too disappointed as we had the letter to examine. We held it up to the light of a lamppost. There seemed to be a pound note and some coins sliding about in it.

"Why would the bishop be giving money to Mrs Devine?"

"It mightn't be coins, they could be holy medals and that rectangle thing could a holy picture like a Mass card," Kait said adding, "Delia's husband Dan died only last week."

"How do you know?"

"Because they live next door to me. Delia and Maggie work in the Wood Hospital so she used to ask Mammy to keep an eye on Dan when they weren't in the house," Kait told us.

"Who's Dan anyway?" I asked.

"Her husband.

"But you said he's dead."

"He is but he wasn't dead when Delia asked Mam to keep an eye on him."

"Well, why didn't you say that before. Was he sick?" Ev asked Kait.

"No, he was dying."

"In bed, in his own house?"

"Ya."

"Then how could he tell you if he wanted anything?"

"Delia left a walking-stick on the bed and told him to wallop the wall to our house if he wanted something."

"If he was dying, what would he want?"

"Water or a sup of tay. A few days before he died, he had the Death Rattle."

"What's that?" Ev wanted to know what the Death Rattle was and so did I.

"The noise people make in their throats when they're dying, like false teeth rattling in a glass of water."

"Did you hear it?"

"A course I did. When he started making it, we kept going in to make sure he was still alive."

"I never heard the Death Rattle, and I could have gone to hear it if you told me about it?" Ev said, very annoyed.

"And why didn't you tell me you want to come?" Kait answered, fed up with Ev's giving out and said to madden her, "It was great craic in the end, Ev."

"How's that?" Ev demanded, not knowing how someone dying could be great craic.

"Because when the priest anointed him, he stopped making the rattle. Delia thought he was nearly dead, so she tied his jaw with a piece of twine."

"Tied his jaw with a piece of twine! Why did she do that?" I asked surprised at such a thing.

"How do I know! It's just something they do. Anyway, as soon as she had the twine tied, didn't Dan's hand start to move. It jerked and jumped a bit and landed on the stick. Delia said you should have seen the way he held on to it and lifted it and banged it against the wall in an awful temper." Delia was petrified. It was Kait's mother who untied the string. Dan let an almighty roar out of him with a real hoarse and raspy voice. 'Musha, aren't ye in a hurry to see me dead. Ye could as least wait until the Banshee came to keen me away.'

"It was then Mammy and Delia realised that he wouldn't die until they heard the Banshee."

"Did she come?"

"The same night, so Mammy laid him out the next morning and they had a wake."

"You never told us," Ev looked at Kait in an aggrieved way.

"Ara! Sure, there was more dogs and cats in the house than people so there was no room for ye."

"You never tell us about the good things ye do," Ev said a bit peeved and then asked, "Who is Mrs Devine anyway?"

"You can see for yourself tomorrow after school when we give her the Bishop's letter."

"The brown and sandy wan said you have to deliver it as soon as possible," Úna reminded Kait.

Ev said getting back on Kait's good side again, "Don't mind her. She must think you're the postman, Kait."

"The bishop's auld housekeeper can say what she likes but I won't be doing her bidding until it suits me. Who does she think she is, anyway, giving me orders?"

The next day after school Úna and Ev came with me and Kait to Kilmartin Road to help us deliver the letter. I ran into Mrs McLoughlin's house to get a few slices of bread and put ham and cheese between them. Kait grabbed a piece of brown bread and butter from her house.

The three of us opened the metal gate and walked to the house and knocked on the door. A small knob of a woman, with butter-blonde hair pulled up in a knot on top of her round, little head opened the door. She had no waist or hips. I suppose she had legs, but she was wearing a wide, flounced skirt that came down to nearly the top of her boots. If she was in a forest in Germany, the other gnomes would think she was an overgrown one of them.

"Howya, Maggie, we got this letter for Delia from a wan in the Legion," Kait said as she handed the letter to the woman who was as wide as the door. Looking over her head, I saw a pile of cats in the hall at the cross-door of the kitchen.

"Maggie, shut that front door or the cats will get out!" we heard a voice say.

"I can't shut the door on the girls' faces."

"Well, tell them to come in. We can't leave Kait Kenny standing on the doorstep after all the help her family gave us when Dan died." We didn't wait for a second chance and skipped into the kitchen and saw the owner of the voice.

She was the complete opposite to Maggie. Tall, big, wide shoulders and brown eyed, dark haired with a bun at the back of her head and not on top like the blonde woman, sitting on a chair near the fire, knitting an Aran jumper.

We couldn't believe our luck. At school, most girls were knitting Aran sweaters or cardigan. The white jackets had become fashionable with the Clancy Brothers and then the American tourists started buying them. My mother and Mrs Curry couldn't believe a woman like Jackie Kennedy would be seen in such an Irish thing as an Aran cardigan. They were used to looking down their noses on people who wore the white woollen clothes. When they were children, it was only the poor who wore home-knitted or home-made garments. They wouldn't show us how to make the cable stiches as it went against their very natures to help their daughters made something they associated with the life they wanted to leave behind.

Úna's and Kait's mothers were too busy with the children, so they couldn't help us either with the tricky, complicated parts where you had to pass the stiches onto the third needle. Even though we knew we'd have no help from our mothers, we bought the needles, wool and patterns and fumbled our way through.

Seeing Mrs Devine with the knitting in her hands, the thought passed through all our heads that we had to flatter her, so she'd help us. Ev picked up a lovely, little ball of ginger fluff. Stroking the kitten, she said, "I wish my mother would let me have a kitten." and asked in a soft voice, "What's this one called?"

"Snowflake," Delia replied.

"How can she be Snowflake if she's orange?" Ev's voice returned to normal.

"It's a he and he's Snowflake because his mother was Snowball."

"Are all of Snowball's kittens called a cold name?" Ev said in a sarcastic tone, but Delia gave her as good as she got.

"No, that one there is Carrot," she said pointing to a black kitten and that there is Chocolate she said pointing to a white kitten and that one with spots is Stripe."

"You have a great imagination, so you do, Mrs Devine."

"It was Maggie's idea and call me Delia, not Mrs Devine."

"Alright. Does Maggie knit too?"

"Ask her yourself, she has a mouth on her." Now we were laughing, delighted with the craic we were having with Mrs Devine.

"Are you knitting that jumper for one of the kittens."

"Indeed, I amn't. Got more fashion sense than to mix fur and wool."

"For the Clancy Brothers, then?"

"When they sing me a song, I'll knit them a jumper."

"We'll sing for you. Ya know some people are knitting jumpers for a woman who pays them because she sells them to Americans," Kait said and handed Delia the envelope. She put it into the pocket of her black skirt, denying us the pleasure of knowing what it was.

"Good for them but I'm knitting this for a lad who was never warm when he was small."

Straightaway Liam came to mind. I wondered where he was and if he was warm. Now he would be big and would look a bit like Cousin Sammy because he had the same colour hair and eyes.

"What song are ye going to sing for me and Maggie?"

"*I'll tell me ma when I go home,*" we chorused, and we started singing. Some of the cats looked at us and others hid under the table. Maggie piled jam onto a big slice of bread and ate it while we sang.

"Ye should have been here the night of Dan's wake to cheer us up."

"Kait never told us about it," Ev said shooting Kait an accusing look.

"Arlene plays the accordion, but Evelyn doesn't," Kait said getting her own back on Ev.

"I miss Jock playing on the Square," Delia said.

I answered, "I remember Jock playing too."

"He'd warm the cockles of your heart," Delia replied but Ev was getting fed up with this musical conversation and said, "There's no market, so what good would it be if he played, there would be no one around to hear him."

"Well, as least he was at Nan Gormley's wake and played," I said and told the two women I might play at the youth club we were starting. Ev butted in to say that we were leaving the Legion and not doing the paper round anymore, and then headed towards the hall, indicating to the rest of us that it was time to go.

"Make sure ye come back and tell us how ye got on," said Delia, coming to the front door with us. Maggie and the dogs trailed behind her.

"We will, you can be sure we will." We meant it because Delia was great craic.

Friday 13th

I woke at eight o'clock. My head was full of worries, thinking that nothing would turn out right on the first night of the youth club. Wondering if I still had the key to open the parish hall door, I jumped out of bed and checked. Then, in a panic, I looked to see if I had the tickets that we'd hand out to the people who came, that is, if anyone came at all.

I imagined the banner Dad had nailed to the top of the stage strewn on the floor, so I dressed real quick and ran up Railway Terence and Hospital Street to the hall. It was still in place. I opened the press under the stage to make sure the record-player was alright.

The chapel bells were ringing for nine o'clock Mass so I decided to go and pray that the Drumbron Youth Club would get off to a good start. On the way to Mass, I met Úna who was going into work in the Quinn's. I made her promise she'd come even if her house went on fire because it would be awful if no one turned up. After Mass, I headed up to Tobair Benin Road to see Nuala. She was as nervous as me about no one turning up. It was only when she said, "At least we know a few like Kait, Úna and my sister Alison will be there. You said your cousin was coming so he will be another one."

It was then I remembered Sammy was coming to visit so I left her and flew home.

His car was parked outside. I rushed in and saw him talking to Mammy. She gave me a cross look. I took no heed of her and joined in the conversation, but she insisted I brushed my hair and tied it back in a ponytail. My hair was the bane of her life.

She told me to go and help Mrs McLoughlin in the kitchen so she could have Sammy all to herself. Dad came home for lunch, and we stayed sitting at the table talking until nearly five. Then I washed and put on my nicest mini-skirt, a white short-sleeved top, and my high heels. Sammy got ready too. Just before seven, he drove me to the parish hall. Nuala, looking fab wearing a mini dress and her hair ironed straight, was already inside as Dad had got a set of keys made for her too.

The hall was ready, decorated with the chains of crepe paper and the banner was nailed onto the top of the stage so there was very little to do. Two chairs were on the stage, one with the record-player and the other right beside it, with the records stacked on it. Sammy said he would use a table instead of two chairs, that way the records could be spread out and their names easily seen.

"Why didn't I think of that?" Nuala said and walked towards a small table by the wall. Sammy followed her and before she could put her hands on the table, he had it picked by the two sides and was carrying it up the steps to the stage. The next minute when I looked, their two bent heads were close together, looking at the records. I hadn't time to think about them because Kait, Úna and Ev were knocking on the door.

They had come to help me which was great because with their eejiting and the silly things they were saying about if the street was empty when we opened the door, we would go and get Legless to come and throw stones at Fr Mannion, I was shaking with laughter and not with nerves.

At half past seven Fr Mannion arrived and gave us permission to open the doors. I gasped and nearly stopped breathing when I saw the big crowd outside.

Putting my fingers to my eyes I pressed really hard because I wanted to cry. Happiness was stuck in my neck in a big lump and only for Úna handing me a roll of tickets I might have let the tears fall. Fifteen minutes of tearing off a ticket and taking the money kept me busy and then things slowed down as the last few lads bought their tickets.

Next thing we knew Fr Mannion was getting on stage, tapping the microphone with his fingers and saying, 'One Two Three.' When he declared the Drumbron Youth Club officially open, the applause that followed was the first music to my ears that night.

Before Fr Mannion left the stage, he said he would be back at half past ten and to make sure we finish up on time. Once he was off the stage, the crowd standing in front of it parted like the Red Sea. The lads went to one side and the girls to the other. Ev was beside me on the stage. She placed the Clancy Brother's record *I'll tell me Ma when I go home* on the plate and then and shouted, "We are townies and we are having a disco, not a dance in a country hall. I want everyone out on the floor for *I'll tell me Ma when I go home* dancing or acting the eejit! When the song is over, you stay where you are and dance with the person next to you. Do ya hear me?"

"We do!" was the crowd's delighted reply, thrilled someone was forcing them to enjoy themselves.

"Well, if I see anyone not doing what I'm telling ye, I'll have my father arrest ye!" which drew a laugh. I was delighted Ev had taken over because I wouldn't have the nerve to talk to a whole room of people, just to put on the records. I had *Puppet on a Sting* in my hand waiting for the Clancy's to finish. Everyone had a great time, and it wasn't until towards the end of the night that the crowd started sitting down, tired out from all the dancing. I hadn't spoken to Nuala all night and wondering where she was, I looked around and saw her by Sammy's side.

Then Fr Mannion appeared out of the blue. The priest gave us a little speech about going straight home and not straying. A voice called out, "But my house is around a corner..." which made us all laugh. Then the hall started to empty.

I was looking towards the door when Nuala's voice said, "Ar, Sam is driving me home. Do you mind if I leave the tidying up until tomorrow?"

"Of course not, Nuala."

"If Mam is still up, I'll bring Sam in to get him to chat to her cos from what he's told me, I think she might know some of the people he knows."

Evelyn who was standing near me said, "Any excuse is a good excuse when it's about holding onto your man."

That left me to walk back to my house, but I didn't mind because I was with Ev, Kait and Úna. We talked about everything that had happened in our first disco. Úna came with us as far as the railway station.

"You can't go up the tracks alone at this time of the night," Kait said with a little tremor in her voice.

"Let's go back through town and we'll walk with you, cos I still want to tell ye about how Rory Callaghan fancies Kait."

We followed Ev's orders because we were too excited to go home. We walked Úna to Dun na Rí Road and stood outside the graveyard talking. Then she insisted on coming with us as far as the Wood Hospital and when we got there, we decided we'd walk her back again but only at far as the post office. With all the talking and walking, it was well after two in the morning when I got home.

I thought I'd be tired, but I couldn't sleep. My mind was busy playing all the songs and the dances, the things the guys had said and the things I had said. It was hard to turn the memories of the night off.

The next morning Dad woke me up with a cup of tea. I sat up half asleep. "What time is it?"

"It's nearly one, lassie."

"It can't be."

"It is but you deserve the rest with all the work you put into making the youth club a roaring success. Everyone is talking about it, wondering why no one ever thought of it before."

"Dad, don't forget you helped me too." I took a sip from the cup and put it on the floor so I could hug Dad around the neck.

"Will you get up so you can say goodbye to Sammy?"

"A course I will," I say rubbing my eyes, "but Dad, the girls were calling him Sam last night."

"Like Sam McGuire? I have no problem with that." Naturally, he wouldn't. Sam McGuire had given his name to the GAA cup that was held aloft very year in Croke Park to the cheers of thousands who loved the game, and my father was among them.

The following legion night we told Miss Kelly we wouldn't be able to attend the meetings anymore as we had study from eight to nine for our Inter Cert. She was very understanding and delighted we were such good students. What she didn't know was that we rarely went to the second study but hung around Castle Fields to talk and so Ev could smoke before we went home. She had started smoking seriously because Ricky smoked and because it was the grown-up thing to do. I tried taking a few puffs, but I nearly coughed my guts out, so I just pretended I was smoking and just brought the fag to my lips but didn't inhale.

Kait didn't even pretend. She said, "I'm never going to smoke. You should see my mother when she's desperate for a cigarette and has no money. She gets nervous and cross with everyone, so she does." Úna agreed with her.

"I haven't a notion of wasting my money on fags. I'd rather buy a bag of chips on the way home."

"I love chips with piles of vinegar," I said.

"Oh, stop it, my belly's rumbling. How much money do you have? Between us all we might have enough for a bag," Ev said jumping off the bridge. We followed behind. Úna, who was still working for the Quinn's in the evening, said she needed her money for nylons.

"I can't wear my lovely high heels if I don't have a decent pair of nylons. I don't know what happens but mine are always getting laddered."

At school we had to wear lace up brogues with thick stockings, but we wore our heels to Mass and the youth club discos which took up most of our time. Every week we went to Nuala's house to decide what records we'd play on the Friday night and talk about what else we could do to make The Youth Club lively and entertaining. Ev, who was full of ideas, said we should have a talent contest after the Christmas holidays. We jumped at the idea without realising how much work it would take to organise it.

Talent Contest

First, the poster had to be painted to announce it.

Second, the 'interviews' with the contestants were complicated. We thought a talent contest was singing or playing a musical instrument but there were all sorts of talents in Drumbron.

We had guys who wanted to do magic tricks, skits, read poetry, dance, imitate the sounds of birds, and another who did cartwheels across the stage.

"This is mad. How can we compare singing to dancing?" Nuala asked.

"Why don't we divide the contest into sections?" Ev suggested.

"Like what?"

"Singing. Dancing."

"That's sounds alright but poetry?"

"Drama for poems and skits."

"And 'Away with The Fairies' for the bird sounds and the cartwheels," Ev said, and we laughed. Nuala said the crazy acts could be called, 'Bewildering Acts.' In the end, Dad told me it could be called Miscellaneous.

After that was sorted, we had to think about the prizes; not knowing if we'd give a prize for every section or only one to the overall winner.

If we had known what we were getting into, we wouldn't never have started. It was too late now, so we had to go ahead with it. Fr Mannion was going to be the judge with Miss Imelda Walsh helping him.

As well as the talent contest, we were still struggling with our Aran jackets – dropping more stiches than we kept on the needles. Sometimes we had to undo the part we had knitted because there were more holes than stitches per square inch but at least Delia helped us a lot with our woollen project. As it was cosy in Delia's, we usually stayed longer than we had intended to because we liked being in Delia's house and might never have left it if it wasn't for the visitors.

Sometimes a man or a woman, who we had never seen in Drumbron, called to see Delia. We seemed to make the visitors uncomfortable because they lowered their eyes and didn't speak when we were about. Sensing they would be more at ease without us in the house, we left but not without giving the visitors dirty looks for taking Delia from us.

Our active lives kept us from studying. Before Christmas, the party we had at the youth club kept us busy. After Christmas it was the talent contest. Then, before Easter, Sam arrived to take Nuala to see Joe Dolan's showband in Sligo. We begged to go too, so Sam squashed us all into his car and we saw Joe sing *Pretty Brown Eyes*. The next time we squeezed into the car, it was to go and hear Dickie Rock and the Miami Showband and another time to see The Miami. If we had a subject about how to squeeze six people into a car or about showbands, we would have been the best in our class at it.

The only kind of school thing we did was to help Ev write letters to Ricky. Our copy books were filled with beautiful phrases and expressions for Ricky, who we knew would not appreciate them. Me and Nuala did drawings of hearts and cupids firing arrows so he would remember he loved her.

In the last term as the Inter Cert exam approached, we reassured ourselves there was still time to study and learn what we needed to pass. Then, all of a sudden, the exam was only three weeks away. In those last few weeks before the Inter Cert, we stayed up late, got up early, sat over books while eating, asked each other questions on the way to school and crammed as much as we could into our heads.

Mrs McLoughlin and Delia said novenas for us, as well as lighting candles. After every exam paper we came out to look at each other and shake our heads, saying it wasn't fair the questions were so difficult, but surprised we were able to answer some of them. We were positive we hadn't passed any of the subjects and walked around down in the dumps but then things started happening and we forgot to worry.

Ricky arrived in Drumbron in a Mini. He wasn't expelled from the school in Enniskillen, so his father bought him a car for being good. Ricky's father might not have been angry with him, but Ev was very angry.

"I don't care if he has a car, I am never going to talk to him again in my life."

"You're only saying that."

"I amn't. How can I talk to him if he never answered any of the millions of letters I wrote him?"

"Well, if he sees you looking so 'Dollybird,' he'll be after you again."

Ev was looking great, wearing a pink mini dress and had her hair like Cilla Black. Her eyes were like a panda bear lined in thick black and her mouth real sexy with pale lipstick. She had four pairs of kitten heels which made her look a little taller. When she walked, she had a sway to her hips, so we'd sing *Get Back* to slag her, but she swayed even more.

Later that same evening we saw a pink flash. It was Ev in Ricky's Mini heading out the Sligo Road.

A few days later when she appeared among us, she said to me, "Ar, if Dad asks if I'm with you, say I am, will you?" Garda

Curry never asked me, thank God, so I didn't have to lie. That summer of 1968 we barely ever saw Ev. It was a pity because it would be the last summer all of our gang would be together.

We were sitting on the wall in Castle Fields when Kait told us she was going nursing to Liverpool. "I'm going nursing this September."

"You can't until you are eighteen."

"I know but I'm doing what Maura McLoughlin did. Two years with the nuns in Liverpool and then I'll start real nursing."

"I don't want you to go."

"Have to."

"At least we'll have summer together, not like last year when you were in Sligo."

"Can't, so I can't. I need to save money for the trip to England, so I told Mrs Jones I'm going back."

The next day Mrs Jones arrived at Kait's house to pick Kait and her suitcase up and drive them to Sligo.

Loretta and Jim Smith

So it was just me, Úna and Nuala who were left in Drumbron for the summer. Nuala and I played tennis, but we weren't the only people on the tennis court that summer. Loretta and her friends were there too and so was Jim Smith. The first time we saw the four of them, we nearly had kittens and pretended we didn't see them, but it was hard not to see. Jim Smith was tall, wearing jeans and a tee-shirt, looking great and the girls were dressed to the nines with the whole, white tennis rig out.

After the Primary Cert, Loretta and her friends had gone away to boarding school, but we saw them sometimes around during the school holidays and seeing Jim Smith with Loretta bothered us. We wondered should we tell Úna. She rarely brought the Quinn kids to Castle Fields because there was another place with sand pits and swings near her house and that is where she went. If we told her, she might tell Kait and break her heart before she went away to Liverpool in September so what good would it do. We didn't say anything, but it weighed heavily on us.

My cousin Sam came for a few days' holidays. He took us for a drive to Ross Point. Another day we asked him to drive to Sligo, so we could pay a surprise visit to Kait. Mrs Jones answered the door and seemed surprised Kait had friends calling. Kait was in the kitchen ironing sheets. We could barely see her behind the big pile she had already done. We asked her would she like to come for a walk with us. Mrs Jones said Kait couldn't take time off.

We were hoping the woman of the house might offer us a cup of tea. She didn't so we left. I was sort of glad in a way because I was afraid I'd let it out that I had seen Jim Smith with Loretta at the tennis court. It was turning out for the best that Kait had gone to Sligo for the summer and was going to Liverpool in September.

Exam Results

Sam hung around Drumbron and spend most of the time with Nuala, so it was he who drove us to the convent the day the Inter Cert results came out. Kait phoned from the guesthouse in Sligo and asked Sr Beatriz to give her results to Úna. Deep down we thought we had failed. We waited worried while the nun fumbled with the list of names looking for ours. Name by name she gave the results.

We had all passed. Unable to believe it, we left in silence. It took until we got to *An Lár* for it to sink in that we had actually passed the Inter Cert. Then as if lightening had stuck, we became electrified, jumping up and down, holding each other around the waist and swinging around in a circle like a sort of a Siege of Ennis dance.

"It's a pity Kait passed," Ev said.

"Why are you saying such a horrible thing?" Nuala demanded to know.

"Because now she will be able to go to Liverpool and not be with us in fifth year."

"You're right," Nuala said. "That means she is going away for keeps."

"A course she is, once she comes from Sligo, she's gone.

"Know what?"

"What?"

"We'll have a special disco in the youth club to celebrate passing our Inter Cert, and we'll make it a farewell party for Kait, too."

"We could have a cake and give her presents."

Nuala cut us short saying, "Oh my God! We left Sam waiting in the car!" and she ran back to the gate on the chapel side of the convent.

Mammy Not Happy

Mammy was disappointed that I didn't get better marks.

"Really, Mary, to think that our cleaning woman's daughter got five honours and you only get one. Your father is going to be very disappointed. He always thought you were so intelligent. I tried to tell him you had to study but he never listened to me."

Dad came home. He was very happy with me and my one honour.

"Are you sure, Dad? Mammy thinks I could have done better."

"Arlene, you are a great lass, one of the founders of the youth club, not many can boast such an achievement."

"But Daddy…"

"Any father would be proud of such a girl as you."

I hugged him, half crying and told him I was sorry I didn't get the honour in art because I wanted to go to art college.

"You'll get one in your Leaving Cert," he reassured me.

"I will, too."

The next day, Mrs McLoughlin told me I was a great girl to get an honour at all because of all the other activities I was involved in.

"But I didn't get five honours like Maura."

"But Maura wasn't wild like you, Mary. She never had the devilment in her that you have."

"You are not disappointed that I don't behave like a good girl?"

"Not for the world, *a grá*. You've a kind heart inside that body that can't keep quiet. I'm telling you, not everyone would talk to Delia like you and your pals do."

"What do you mean, Mrs McLoughlin?

"You know Delia has no family of her own?"

"She does. Sometimes people from England or America come to see her."

"They are the babies she minded in the Home. They come to see the only woman who gave them a bit of love when they were small."

"I didn't know that."

"Well, now you do but don't be saying anything. Delia mightn't like people to know she was reared in a Home."

"A course I won't."

Then she told me Maura was nearly finished her training and she would qualify as a nurse very soon.

Summer Ends

The summer was ending. At the beginning of September, we said goodbye to Kait at the station. I felt the same sort of sadness I had felt when Brigid and Liam disappeared around the time of Storm Debbie, which left so much damage around town.

When Kait got on the train and put her face to the pane of glass like Martin Ward used to do when we were small, I spread my lips around my teeth and made a pretend smile forcing myself to be cheerful. This gesture pushed my lower eyelids upwards and kept the tears inside from spilling out.

The train was taking one of my best pals away. The girl who been beside me since we were small, who called me Arlene, who knew about my baby brother in the shoebox, who sat near me on the bad side with the Home Babies, who knew the sins I told in my First Confession. She had been part of me and now she was going far away.

'Why do you have to go, Kait? Why can't you stay and let things be like they always were? Come back, don't go, stay with me!' my mind screamed as the train pulled out.

When it was out of sight, I stopped waving and lowered my hand to wipe my nose. The tears must have fallen inwards to my nostrils because clear water was dripping from them. My throat was sore and making gasping sounds. The three of us left the station with our heads low. None of us spoke until we got to *An Lár*.

Outside Wynn's Bakery, Nuala said, "Wonder what fifth Year will be like?"

"We'll have to study and not leave things til the last minute like we did in Inter," I said.

"So the day after tomorrow we'll be wearing our shitty uniforms again," Ev said.

"I won't be," Úna said. "I'm not going back to school."

"You can't do that, Úna!" I cried out.

"I have to. Ye know the factory closed."

The factory that had opened when we were in the primary school was closing. They had been laying off people for the last few months. Úna's father was the first to go. I heard Mr Delaney saying he was a troublemaker and that he should have been grateful for the few years' work he got from factory, instead of protesting about how the factories were getting tax breaks and then clearing off.

"Yeah, but what's that got to do with you leaving school?"

"Dad can't get a job. He was looking all summer. Poor Mam has to scrimp and scrape to make ends meet."

"He can go to England on the boat like the other fathers," I said.

"He can't. Mammy won't let him. She wants him at home with her."

"But where will you get a job?" Nuala asked.

"The Quinn's. They want me to work in the shop. Mrs Quinn will teach me how to do the books and how to order the things from the salesmen who come in."

"But who'll mind the Quinn kids?"

"My sister will, and Mrs McKenna will still keep the house clean."

My world was falling apart. Ever since I can remember, the sun rose every morning, stayed in the sky alone or behind clouds, telling me it was day or night. Kait and Úna were my daylight. We were part of each other. Now one part of me was going far away and the other was separating from me. I didn't want this to happened. I wanted my two sister-friends to stay at home, in the place where we had always been. Evelyn was the only one was still herself, with the stupid remarks coming out of her mouth all the time.

"The McNultys and the Quinns are joined together like Siamese Twins," she said but for once she didn't sound funny to me.

I said, "Bye. See ye two at school. I'll see you around, Úna." I rushed off because my voice was full of tears, and I was mad with Úna and wanted to shout at her.

When I got home, I rushed upstairs and threw myself on my bed and cried and cried, my body heaving up and down. I must have fallen asleep because the next thing I heard was Mammy parking the car. She opened the front door and said, "Mary, are you in? Why didn't you put the light on?"

I didn't answer.

She came up the stairs and pushed my door opened. "What are you doing in the dark?"

"Nuthin," I mumbled.

"Nuthin? The word is nothing. It is about time you started speaking properly and not like the people of Drumbron."

I didn't answer.

She put the light on.

I screamed at her to turn it off.

"Your father is going to hear about the way you are behaving. It's fine for the experts to say teenagers are moody, but I see boldness."

"Mam, leave me alone! I want to sleep."

"You didn't have your supper."

"I amn't hungry."

"When I was young, I never spoke to my mother the way you are speaking to me. Your father is going to hear about it as soon as he comes home."

"I don't care."

At last she left. I couldn't go back to sleep. Getting up quietly so Mam wouldn't hear me, I picked up the book that Kait and I had started reading. It was a habit we had since we were small to get the same book and after reading each chapter, we'd talk about it before we went on to the next one. It made me cry, so I put Tom Jones' *The Green, Green Grass of Home* on the record-player Dad had bought me. While it was playing, I saw Nan and Nanny's house with the grass growing wild around where the chickens used to be and Nan swishing them away with the twig. I pulled the needle off the record.

At that moment, the door opened a little and Dad said, "Do you mind if I come in, Arlene?"

I didn't answer.

He took it for a yes because he was standing inside the door looking at me. "What's the trouble, Missy?"

"Nuthin."

"I heard the wee Kenny lass went to England today."

I turned and looked at him.

"It's hard when a friend goes away," he said.

I never knew that he knew that Kait and I were friends but then, he was a Garda, and the Gardaí knew everything. Without realising it, I was in his arms sobbing my heart out. He didn't say anything until I stopped, worn out with no more tears left in me. Then he said, "Why don't you write to her and send the letter first thing tomorrow morning, so she gets it soon."

"Dad, I never thought of that."

"She'll be delighted to know you are thinking of her."

"I'm thinking of her and missing her so much, Daddy."

"You can be sure she'll be missing you too and everyone in Drumbron."

"Daddy, you're right. I'll tell her everything that's happening, so she won't be lonely."

"That's my wee lass."

I hugged Daddy and said, "You are the best Daddy in all Ireland, England and broad Scotland."

Letters to Kait

I wrote telling her how I barely ever saw Úna or Nuala. Then so as not to sound too much of a *beál bocht* I told her about Batt the postman. We used to laugh because when he had juicy news, he would stand right up in front of you and say, 'Come here, come here,' even though he had his face inches from yours and you couldn't get nearer. Knowing that would make her laugh, I told her how he had said to my mother, 'Come here, come here! Did ya hear what happened to that young Martin lad?' and filled a page about Ricky crashing the car.

'Kait, can you imagine what a desperate chancer Ricky is? He gets a car for not being expelled from school and crashes it and he's not a bit bothered! Ev is nearly as bad. I mean, I thought she'd be hanging around with me now that the car is in the garage but no, she spends all her time in Castle Fields with Ricky and his pals, playing cards, smoking and drinking.' I posted the letter the next day and crossed my fingers she'd write back soon and filled the emptiness.

1969-1972

During the summer of 1969, as my life was unravelling and my friends slipping away, I was glad my cousin Sam was staying us. Even though Evelyn said he spoke like a newspaper, and he spent most of the time with Nuala, I liked to see him in the kitchen when I got up.

"Arlene, there's a protest outside the GPO in Dublin tomorrow. Nuala and I are driving up," he told me one morning as I poured water into the teapot.

"Are ye? Tomorrow, is it?" I answered half asleep.

"Yes. We firmly believe the Irish Government must act to stop the atrocities."

In the North, the people who considered themselves Irish and were known as Nationalists were being attacked and burned out of their homes.

I sat down before I answered him. "I'm going too."

"That's what I was expecting you to say."

"Of course I'm going. Mr McNulty says it is getting to the stage where no one is safe from being murdered," I replied.

"Úna's father has a point. The situation is untenable." Sam and Mr McNulty always seemed to agree on things about the North even though they were completely different from each other in other aspects.

The GPO

I went with them and joined the thousands who gathered outside the GPO – the iconic building, where in 1916 a group of Irish men and women had proclaimed the thirty-two counties of Ireland a Republic. We gathered in the same spot to let the Irish living in the six counties on the British side of the border know they were not alone. That part of Ireland had remained in the UK after the Irish War of Independence that took place at the beginning of the twentieth century. The Irish won the war but lost six of its thirty-two countries. In 1922 Ireland was partitioned, leaving two thirds of the province of Ulster under English rule.

During that war in 1922, news travelled slow. Now the events from the North were in our kitchen as soon as they happened. We sat in front of the television and saw people, who lived a few miles above our town, being attacked and terrorised.

We devoured the news about Derry and Belfast and people like Bernadette Devlin. She was a young girl who could have been on *Top of the Pops* with her mini skirt and her long, hippy hair swinging from side to side. She moved in her feisty fashion, like Evelyn did. For a tiny girl she was amazingly brave, letting nothing faze her – a modern Irish warrior, a *Gráinne Mhoal*, a Queen Maeve or a Countess Markiewicz.

We read every article we could lay our hands on about the youngest member of the English Parliament ever elected. We didn't move from in front of the telly when we saw her face on the screen, listening to every word she said, telling the world things had to change in the North of Ireland. Evelyn loved the pint-sized girl, small like herself and unstoppable. She never tired of telling us, "I told ye good goods come in small packages. Wait and see how I become a politician too and shake the Dáil up!"

At the beginning of August, the radio and television held us captive as we listened to what was happening.

"They are always talking about the Bogside. What a funny name to call a place," I said.

"The Bogside! Must be where the Irish were forced to live after the Plantation?" Ev said.

"Yeah, I remember learning how O'Neill and O'Donnell and ninety-nine of his followers cleared off to the continent and left the ordinary people to be thrown off their lands into the bogs," I said.

"No, Sam-know-it-all said the O'Neill and O'Donnell chieftains went to the continent to seek help to continue the war against the English," answered Ev and I was glad Nuala wasn't around to hear her call Sam a know-it-all.

"Anyway, are the ones who are looking for civil rights the descendants of those who had to live in the bogs?" I asked.

"Suppose so because they are living in the worst part of Derry, all lumped up together."

"And now they are not safe. They are being beaten like animals on the civil rights marches and their houses are being set on fire. Úna's father says the RUC are not doing anything to stop the attacks, so himself and another few men are going up to help them," I told her.

"Why don't we go too?" said the dare-devil who was always willing to do anything.

"Good idea. Would Ricky drive us up?"

"He would if the Mini wasn't still in the garage getting fixed." He had practically wrecked the Mini. He had been drunk when driving.

"But isn't it ready yet?"

"No way! They have to wait for the parts to come from Dublin and it will take a while yet."

"Just our luck not having the car when we need it."

"And you wouldn't mind but I could drive us to Derry. Ricky is teaching me."

"Is he? I'd love to know how to drive."

"It's dead easy. Ask your father to teach you."

"I will when he gets back from wherever he is." Daddy was away a lot because of the Troubles in the North.

"Sure why don't we go to the station and inquire about buses to Derry?"

"Yeah, all we have to do is go to Sligo and from…" I couldn't finish the sentence because Mammy was pulling Evelyn up from the chair.

"What is this I hear, Miss Curry, about you going to Derry? The only place you are going is home. When I'm finished with this girl here, I'll be over to tell your mother about what ye're planning to do!" Mammy was beside herself with rage, pushing Evelyn towards the door. Then she turned on me and started shouting. "God between us and all harm, Mary but this is a fine state of affairs to hear the child I nursed at my breast speaking like a lunatic. *Tá tUltán de chac.*" In her anger, she had dropped her refined Gay Byrne way of speaking and sounded like she used to do when I was small. She saw me edging my way towards the door and blocked me.

All I could do to get away from her was to take a few steps backwards towards the dresser. I stood staring at her as defiant as I could. "Mammy, I only said the RUC and B Specials were right savages the way they attack the people."

"Musha," Mammy looked pityingly at me, "what would you know about that?"

"I was only…"

"Going to cause trouble like the Ultains always did. I don't know where I went wrong with you, but you can be sure Evelyn's mother will be hearing about yer plans of going to Derry."

"But Mammy…"

"I'll put paid to your stupidity. By God you'll wait a long time before you see another penny coming out of my purse. I'll knock sense into you if it's the last thing I do."

"I can always thumb to Derry."

She came close to my face. I tried to look brazen, but I was frightened and lowered my eyes.

"You attempt to do anything like that, and I'll have you locked up in a convent. And it won't be as a boarder." She had told me a few times about wild girls from her own homeplace in Connemara who wouldn't leave the men alone. They were locked up in laundries for their own good, so I knew what she meant. She was holding me by the shoulders, her nails clawing into my flesh pushing my back hard against the dresser.

"What were you saying about getting a bus to Derry?"

"I was only codding about going to Derry."

"That better be the truth. I'll be keeping my eye on you and if you take one step wrong, you'll know what the inside of a laundry looks like."

"Daddy, wouldn't let you…"

"Daddy," she spat the word out, "is too busy helping Miss Imelda Walsh get a job in Dublin and God knows what else she and he are doing."

I didn't know why that made her furious. Lots of people went to Daddy or another garda for references for a job or when they needed to get a passport, so why was she angry. I tried to step sideways, but the movement drew her eyes, wild in her head, to my hair. An image of her with scissors in her hands flashed through my mind. I pushed my hair behind my ears and promised to be good saying.

"Mammy, I'm sorry. Ev and I were just talking, nothing else."

"Good. Now start acting like I want you to."

"I will, I promise."

"What are you promising?"

"I am going to study and get good results in my Leaving."

"I'm telling you it's hard lines when the cleaning woman's daughter can pass with more honours than my daughter."

"Maura only did her Inter. I'll be doing my Leaving which is harder."

"Whatever exam she did, she got better marks than you, so less ould buck. Do you hear me? Well, heed me or you'll be the sorry girl."

I nodded my head. I knew I had to behave because Mammy forgot I existed until something went wrong. Then she blew up and took her anger out on me like she was doing now.

Mammy wasted no time in going to the Curry's house and telling Ev's mother about how we were planning on going to the Bogside in Derry. Mrs Curry told Ev she was not allowed out in the evenings for a month and there was no pocket money either.

Neither things bothered Evelyn. For years she had been going out through the bedroom window and sliding down the drainpipe. She didn't give a sugar if she got pocket money or not, as she had another way of getting it.

Ricky's father, Mr Martin the local TD, was involved with the Department of Transport, Tourism and Sport. He made sure people knew he was the reason state funding was available for the local club and that it was thanks to him, Drumbron football stadium was one of the first pitches in the county to have floodlights and shower facilities. Therefore, when Ricky and Ev showed interest in helping the local club, the committee were delighted to have the TD's son and a Garda's daughter as raffle-ticket sellers. Ricky left the bookkeeping to Ev as she told him about how she had learned to keep accounts in our Legion of Mary days when we did the newspaper round.

Naturally, the committee never considered checking the amount of tickets sold and the amount of money handed in, which suited Ev fine and kept her in pocket money.

I, on the other hand, couldn't get any money. Daddy was my bank but as he was away in Dublin with his new job, I was skint. I wasn't able to go to the Odeon to see *The Italian Job* or *Hello Dolly*. I was as poor as Kait and Úna used to be, and on top of that, I had to behave like a 'nice girl,' having learned a long time ago it was better not to say what I thought around my mother, so to avoid anything escaping from my mouth, I spent most of the time in Úna's house.

In the middle of August, flashes of the Apprentice Boys Parade were shown on the news. It made Mr McNulty sizzle with rage, so I told him it was a very special day for me because when I was small, I had gone plenty of times with my father to see the parade and to listen to the bands.

"We don't have them parades in this part of the country. Arlene, are you sure it was the Apprentice Boys Parade?"

"I think so because in was in summer when we were on holidays in Cavan."

"Could be alright. They have them parades in Donegal, as well as Cavan and maybe in Monaghan."

"It used to be lovely, Mr McNulty. The streets were always thronged with people, so I used to hold Daddy's hand while we watched it."

"Listening to the marching bands and big drums."

"That's right and the accordions. But what I loved best was the huge banner with golden tassels all around King William."

"Is that right?" he said and gave me a look as though he had seen me for the first time in his life.

"The King has lovely, curly hair and looks so handsome riding his horse with his hand on his hip."

Mr McNulty fixed me with an unblinking look, so I didn't tell him how my eyes used to open wide in delight at the marching bands and how my feet vibrated to the music of the drummers, pipers and accordion players, wanting to follow the parade. If he had known I had been in an Orange Hall, I wonder what kind of queer looks he would have given me.

"Well Arlene, I can tell you the people who lived in the Bogside didn't enjoy the parades."

"But parades are nice, Mr McNulty. I like the St Patrick's Day one here too."

"Of course they are if they are kept to the main street."

"The one I saw in Cavan was in the middle of town."

"That's fine but when the bands file past the homes of our people in Derry, it is to rub it into their faces that they are less than the ones banging the drums."

"That's a pity because the music is lively and stirs you up."

"It is but if it's going past your house all day, it's another story."

"I suppose so."

"Will you be going to Cavan this time too?"

"We don't go now because Dad's new job keeps him in Dublin most of the time. My mother never liked the marching bands or me playing the accordion."

"A wise woman," he said. Úna's younger brother and sister were in the kitchen, so I suppose that's why he never said anything about 'sticking the parades up their *thóins*.' He just said, "things are going to get bad once the marching season started in earnest."

He was right. They did.

On the night of the 11th of August 1969 the residents of the Bogside built barricades around their neighbourhood, so the parade couldn't pass through the streets.

The next morning uniformed men in riot helmets and holding metal shields broke through the barricades, charging against the people. They swarmed through, beating anyone they found on the streets.

Panic spread through the neighbourhood with people fearing for their lives. While some locals fled through any open door they saw, hoping to get away from the police who were armed with batons and pickaxes, others were fighting back using stones and petrol bombs.

The attacks on civilians by the B Specials and RUC police force were so vicious that the Taoiseach, Jack Lynch, said the Irish Government could no longer stand by and see innocent people injured.

Appearing on television, Jack Lynch called for the United Nations to deploy peacekeeping forces to the North. While he waited for the answer to his request, he ordered the Irish Army to set up refugee camps as well as army field hospitals along the border in County Donegal, near Derry, for the Irish from the North who were forced to flee their homes.

Mammy and Mr Delaney were against the idea, saying Lynch was deluded. They were outraged thinking people would be living rent-free and getting meals for nothing. On the other hand, Sam and Nuala wanted to help. They were going to the camp in Donegal. I told them I wanted to go too.

If Mammy knew I was going to the North with Nuala when I got into Sam's car, she pretended she didn't, because she always flattered my cousin and never said anything that could be seen as criticism. I was buzzing with happiness as we headed for Bundoran, a sort of holiday place where we could walk on the beach and eat ice-cream and have bags of chips soaked in vinegar. While Sam and Nuala were having their usual, serious type of conversations I was singing *We're all going on a summer holiday* which dried on my lips when we arrived at what was a scene from a war film. Buses jammed with women and children were arriving at the army camp. Weary, bloodstained people were alighting, grateful for the sandwiches and cups of tea.

Sam mingled with the Derry people, asking them questions about what had happened. Most spoke about the stench of the CS gas and sand-papery feeling it left in your throat. I was stunned when I heard an old man say he had feared for his life.

"We were hiding in the house when we heard death banging on the door." The poor old man had stumbled as fast as his thin legs would take him to the front door and pressed his body against it. His wife leaned the weight of her frail body to his, hoping to keep the door from being bust opened.

On the outside, the soldiers pounded with rifle butts and used their heavy boots to kick at it. The door creaked and strained under the attack. The man saw the wood was going to splinter and break as the hinges jerked, coming loose. He told his wife to get away as he feared any second the door would come crashing down on top of them. Just as they were withdrawing, stumbling shakily away down the hall, the back door opened. Men poured into the house and the hall became filled with neighbours pushing against the door and holding it up. The soldiers kept pushing but the human bulwark held the door fast against the invaders.

The young boys wanted to tell their story, boasting about how brave they had been. The words tumbled out of their mouths as they told Sam how they had helped the big people tear up pavement to have stones to throw at the police.

The girls, not to be outdone, told how they had gathered all the glass bottles they could and gave them to their mammies who were making petrol bombs. From what I gathered the whole of the Bogside was like a war zone.

People armed themselves with clubs and hurls and walked up and down behind the barricades. Men patrolled the area with walkie-talkies communicating with each other, letting people know where help was needed.

A radio station was broadcasting, so that the men and women, who were resisting and fighting to protect their neighbourhood, would be informed about what was happening. Frightened residents were reassured when news reached their ears telling them where their family members were.

First-aid stations had been set up for the injured. They were manned by doctors and nurses.

The people under siege decided it was safer to evacuate the women, children and older people from the danger, even if it meant they had to leave their homes. These vulnerable people were hurriedly put on the buses that were now arriving at the refugee camp in Bundoran. There were so many coming that the Army decided to move some to an army barracks in Longford.

Sam was in the midst of this dreadful scene, moving about talking to people and taking notes for the student newspaper he helped publish. He was very impressed with the great job the army were doing and said that news would make the front page.

Nuala was helping him with interviews while I hung around as shocked and pale as the refugees, more of a nuisance than a help, dumbstruck, unable to do anything. While I marvelled at the strength and courage of those fleeing from the terror of Derry, my own body was reacting badly.

My stomach was heaving with the urge to vomit, and I wanted to hold my splitting head with my hands, but I didn't feel I could afford the luxury of acting the drama queen amidst the deep suffering I was witnessing. People were hurrying about the camp helping others while I was standing still in the way of those who were useful. Sam passed by me and saw the state I was in. He put his arms around my shoulders and led me back to where the car was parked and opened the back door so I could sit on the seat.

"Oh Sam, I feel so guilty for being such an eejit."

"The shock has left you in no condition to help anyone."

"But Sam…"

"Look, not everyone is made of the same stuff and there are other things you can do."

"Like what?"

"Go home and talk to people. Tell them what you have seen, write to the newspapers, collect clothes, books, chocolate and sweets and make parcels and send them to the camps."

The following morning Sam got me a lift back to Drumbron.

I did all that he had told me to do but still felt guilty and wished I was like Nuala.

The Saviours Arrive
On the 15th of August, I was in Úna's house when the news about the British Troops arriving in the North was broadcast. Relief made our shoulders droop, smiles loosened our mouths and contentment spread through the kitchen as we gazed at the soldiers on the TV screen. They had arrived to protect the people.

Mr McNulty said, "I never thought I'd see the day I'd be glad to see English soldiers on the streets of an Irish town but if they protect the people from the B Specials, they can stay as long as they like."

"I wouldn't mind giving a cup of tea to some of the gorgeous-looking lads. Why do uniforms always make fellows look hunky and handsome?" Ev said as we looked at the young English soldiers in plumed berets. They carried low-slung rifles and looked really sexy and breath-taking as they sauntered through the stone-strewn streets.

Later when she told Ricky about the guys in uniform, he said he would dress up in his boy scout outfit if a man in uniform turned her on.

"What did you say?" I asked, laughing at Ricky's antics and wondering if he had been thrown out of the scouts too.

"That he could show his knock-knees and hairy legs to Miss Kelly because I don't want them."

On the television we saw the handsome, young English soldiers walking through the streets and heard the sighs of the pretty, young Irish girls who, like Ev, thought they were gorgeous and fell hard for them.

Mr McNulty said, "Isn't it grand to see an army truck outside the house of a girl waiting for her to come out and not be outside to arrest anyone."

People relaxed in the Nationalist areas. While the girls went out with the soldiers, the mothers made tea and sandwiches for the 'bringers of peace.'

The handsome uniformed heroes shone brightly until, as my cousin, in Sam-speech, informed us that the Native Irish realised the soldiers were there to keep the established order of the British Empire and not to protect them.

As check points and armed soldiers became the norm in Derry and Belfast, Irish people walked in fear, knowing they could be stopped, searched and taken off in army lorries. Their cities were occupied by foreign soldiers and not by 'bringers of peace.'

The force and might of the Crown, dressed in uniform, controlled the Nationalist community. As my cousin Sam said, "the Nationalists would always be the enemy of the Crown. The part of the population that saw itself as British would be the friend."

Gradually the honeymoon came to an end. Young National lads were being shot and killed in safe havens in their own areas – known only to the local communities – where they could go to have a bit of craic without being harassed. The wise heads in the neighbourhoods saw that the loose, innocent talk of the girls was the reason their territory was becoming known to the outsiders who invaded and killed their young men and made life perilous for people living within those areas.

As in every war, the community under siege forbade their women folk to fraternise with the enemy. They warned them not to engage with the soldiers because love is blind, and love is giving. Those who were too much in love to see how dangerous pillow-talk can be had their hair cut or their heads shaved and were ordered to leave the country.

Mr McNulty explained that when the people of the community had evidence against girls and knew that because of them, a Nationalist have been shot or imprisoned, the girls were tarred and feathered as a warning to others. Úna and I shuddered at this treatment of the girls, but we didn't live where armed soldiers walked the streets.

Mr McNulty had been in Derry and saw how the Irish were being treated like criminals in their own country and he was not going to stand idly by. There were other people around town who felt the same as Mr McNulty. They met and got organised, like the Irish had done for centuries, to fight the enemy. Meetings took place in various locations. The chapel was one of those places. Men who hadn't set a foot inside the church for years became regular Mass-goers and the last Mass on Sundays was crowded. In the enclosed, glass-panelled section of the chapel, just in from the entrance, with the fancy name of narthex, was where Mr McNulty arranged to meet the men. Women also spoke to him before entering and sitting in the main body of the church. Unlike me, they weren't afraid.

I kept my head down and my mouth shut because I didn't want to anger Mammy. While my cousin and Nuala stated their opinions in a loud voice, wrote to the newspapers and organised student protests, I was always busy and for first time in my life I wished it was time to go back to school.

September 1969

My first day in fifth year was a lonely day. Whereas other years I had leaped out of bed, dressed and raced down the stairs, shoved something into my mouth, grabbed my schoolbooks and bounced out the door to join Evelyn and Kait at the corner of Sligo Road and Railway Terrace. This year the street would be empty with no one waiting for me, not even Evelyn.

On Friday she had told me, "Just imagine, Ar, me and Ricky will be able to see each other every single minute of every single hour of every single day of the week."

"You can't. We are starting school on Monday."

"I know that, but still, don't wait for me in the morning."

"You can't skip school."

"I can because as Ricky said, while the weather is fine, we should make the most of it."

"But…"

"Look, we have all winter for school and study."

"Your mother will be mad if she finds out."

"She won't know because I am pretending I'm leaving the house early to go to the eight o'clock Mass."

"Ev, your mother knows you don't give a sugar about going to Mass," I exclaimed knowing her mother would not be so gullible as to believe such nonsense.

"I told her I think I have a vocation and need to pray about it."

"You! A vocation! No one will believe that. You'll get caught if you don't go to school."

"I won't cause I'll go to most classes during the week, I'll just be missing some Mondays and Fridays."

"So I won't see you on Monday?"

"Maybe Tuesday. I'm off to the races in Roscommon with Ricky on Monday."

"Isn't Ricky going back to school in Enniskillen?

"He's not. Isn't it great, he's staying here!"

"I thought Mr Martin bought Ricky the car because he wasn't expelled from the posh college in the North."

"That's right. Everything was grand until Mr Martin got the phone call from the headmaster."

"Phone call?"

"Yeah, the one saying the cleaning staff had found a pile of empty whiskey bottles at the back of Ricky's wardrobe."

"How did they know they were Ricky's? Sure, anyone could have left them there?"

"Of course they knew it was him. Anyone would cop on and realise that Ricky's bouts of vomiting and being too sick to leave his bed were hangovers."

"So what's going to happen?"

"As they don't want him back in the school, the father says Ricky will stay here where his mother can keep an eye on him."

"And the car? Is his father taking it off him?"

"No way, Ricky told his mother he needs it for school."

"For school! But sure even the two lay teachers don't have cars."

"I know but it's for us, so we can go places. Like the races."

On the first day of school in September while Ev was in Ricky's car on her way to the Roscommon Races, I was dragging my feet along Railway Terrace with a lump in my throat and tears in my eyes looking at a world that had emptied of everyone I thought would be by my side always.

Ev was gone with Ricky. Kait was in Liverpool nursing. Úna was in the Quinn's getting the children ready for school. I was walking alone instead of linking Kait and Ev's arms like we always did, throwing words at each other until we got to *An Lár* where Úna would be waiting. I was so lost in my grief that I didn't notice Nuala until she called my name.

"Saw Úna this morning, Ar. She's hoping to see you this evening so you can tell her about school. Look, I got a letter from Sam. He's coming this weekend."

After the holidays Sammy had gone back to Trinity College but came to Drumbron at the weekends to see Nuala. It was great Sam was coming even though he spent most of the time in Nuala's house, which was so different from his own beautiful house in Cavan.

Nuala's house was the same type of house as Kait, Úna and Delia's. The front of the house had a big square window downstairs and two smaller ones upstairs. A path in the middle of the garden led up to the front door. There was a hall behind this door. On the right-hand side was a stairs with a wooden banister going up to a landing and the two top bedrooms.

You couldn't see the underneath part of the stairs because a panel of wooden boards hid it. On the other side of the boards was the coalhouse where people kept the coal, turf or sticks for the fire in the kitchen.

Nuala's parents slept in the bedroom on the left-hand side of the hall. It had the big, square window that looked out onto the front garden.

Right at the end of the hall, there was the cross door that lead to the kitchen. That's where me and Nuala spent our time listening to the radio and watching Top of the Pops. There were two doors in the kitchen, the one across from the range leading to the scullery. Some people called the scullery the back kitchen because there was a deep, square, delph sink where you washed the potatoes and did the wash up after dinner. Nuala's mother washed the clothes in the sink with a washing board. The scullery had a window and a backdoor leading out to the yard.

When we were small and put plays on in Kait's house, we used to use the scullery as our dressing room, so we could come out the back door dressed in our costumes.

The other door lead to the lavatory where the McCabes washed their hands and face in the small sink stuck on the wall under a mirror. Nuala's father used the handbasin for shaving. The lavatory, with the long chain, was under a small window so you could open it to let the smells out.

Mr McCabe, who used to sit by the fire in the range while we were at the big, wooden kitchen table, drawing the posters for the youth club or ironing Nuala's hair straight, was always shouting, "Close that door, there a draught!" when we left the toilet door open. The kitchen had lino on the cement floor which would have shocked Mammy more than she was already shocked.

"I am very surprised at the interest Sammy is showing for that girl Nuala. With him coming down from Cavan any chance he gets. How can he see anything in a girl living in a council house?"

"You know, Dervla, her father is on the dole since they closed the beef factory."

"Is that right, John? But that factory closed last year."

"That's how long I'm seeing him at the dole office. Your man who runs the office says Mr McCabe is desperate for work, but it can't be got."

"William told me the new textile factory they opened is closing too."

"I raised the matter at the council meeting the other night."

"Anyway John, forget about the council for a minute and just tell me, what does Sammy see in that girl?"

"She's pretty with a nice figure."

"John, there are far prettier girls than her who don't live in council houses, so why is he so smitten with her?"

"It could have something to do with her mother being a Protestant. They like to marry into their own."

"That is not always the case, John, as you well know."

"William did what many men would like to do. The Pope himself would have left the Vatican if he had seen you."

"Oh, John!"

The pair of them made me sick. My mother was so shallow. It never crossed her mind for a minute that people could like each other for other reasons than where they lived and who they were.

Just as Ev and Ricky were similar in that they were right devils and would do anything, Nuala and Sammy also had a lot in common. Both of them were into history, literature and the Irish language. Ev used to say, "That pair of arty-farties think they are Maud Gonne and Yeats." She was right. Sam was so intellectual that he bored everyone to death except Nuala. Ricky was too wild but not for Evelyn.

There was someone for everyone except me and Úna. We were a pair of lone birds in love with no boy and spending our evenings together in her house.

I had Kait but only in her letters. Batt had bought me the first letter two weeks after she left.

Dear Ar,

I met a lovely lad on the train. He goes to Uni and was telling me about his exams. He wanted the address of the hospital where I'm going but I am no more interested in him than I am in the man on the moon. Jim is the only one I will ever love.

The boat was terrible. Downstairs there was a bar where a lad was singing, but I was as sick as a pig below deck, so I went up the wooden steps to the top part where there's a sort of bench seat. I was hoping the fresh air would help but all it did was blow through me and make my teeth chatter.

Every time the boat swayed and rocked, my stomach heaved, and dirty stuff came up my throat. I felt the bar of chocolate and bag of Tayto swirling around and leaping up. The sour taste of the horrid mixture filled my mouth, so I ran to the side and leaned over to vomit into the sea. My lovely hat that Mammy bought me fell off. The fish must be wondering if it's a boat for leprechauns.

Arlene, I was wondering if you can do me a favour. I forgot to tell you about Mrs Lynch. She lives a few doors up from our house and I go to see her every now and then because she never goes outside the door. The poor woman is always stuck in the house. She used to be delighted when I called to see her. So if you wouldn't mind going to see her sometime, I'd be grateful and if you can't, it doesn't matter because I'll write to her anyway.

Is there any news of Jim? I wonder if he knows I'm gone away. If you hear anything, let me know.

When I arrived late yesterday evening, the nuns in this place told me there was rosary in the chapel, meaning they expected me to go. They are very strict and cross-looking.

I started working this morning and the nuns gave me a lovely uniform. I look like a real nurse with the puffy short sleeved blouse and a white apron but I'm emptying bed pans, making beds and feeding auld gummy wans who can't hold the spoon themselves.

I got your letter and couldn't stop laughing thinking of Batt and his stupidity with his 'Come here, come here.'!

Write soon again and tell me everything.

I'm so lonely without ye to talk to but as least nearly all the girls are Irish, so I'm sure I'll get on with them. Goodbye and God bless.

All my love and kisses,

Your ever-loving friend,

Kait XXXXXXXXXXXXXX (My hand is tired, so I can't write you any more kisses)

Our letters would keep us close, but it wasn't the same as being able to turn and whisper something in her ear while we were at class or walking down the street.

Three short years ago Kait, Úna and Evelyn had been by my side as the four of us ventured through the grey sepulchral door of the convent, hiding the fear we felt behind our bravado giggling. After that first morning, we met on *An Lár* every day. We walked into school brazen as brass, letting nothing worry us, because being together made us strong.

Three years that went too soon. Now I'm alone, except for Nuala. As she and I walked up Church Street and passed through the gate that had looked so daunting only three years ago, I longed for that time and my friends with an ache in my heart.

Fifth Year

Being in fifth year made the younger girls look up to us and made the teachers treat us less like children and more like adults who would soon be working.

Most of the town girls spoke of going nursing or teacher-training, while the country girls were doing to do the exams to enter the civil service as post office clerks or telephonists when they finished their Leaving.

Nuala wanted to study literature at university but knew her parents couldn't afford it, so she was going to become a librarian, which, she said, would give her time to be among books.

Ev used her so-called vocation as an excuse to be with Ricky but some boarders were genuinely interested in entering the religious life. The rest of us in class knew which ones the nuns had seen as potential candidates by the way they doted on them.

Those maybe-nuns were the favourites and could do no wrong. If they were weak in any subjects, they were given grinds, so as to do well in the exams for the training college for teachers in Limerick or for Cathal Brugha College in Dublin.

The girls in A-class had higher ambitions, wanting to study medicine or law and that was the reason they were doing honours in most subjects, while we in B-class only did honours in the subjects we excelled in.

No one in my class spoke of going to university except me. Without Úna and Kait around, I only had the light of going to college at the end of two years to keep me going. I wanted to do Fine Arts and become an artist. It would be difficult to get Mammy to give her consent as she thought a good marriage was the best option for a young lady. However, I hoped that if she saw I was being good, she'd let me go to college.

At school, I was sitting beside the foxy-haired Catherine from Sand Hills. She was very quiet and didn't budge, so there was no whispering behind our hands or passing notes to each other. As I couldn't be up to any devilment, all I could do was to listen to the teachers, go to early study period from five to seven, come home for my tea and go back to late study period from eight to nine. I met Nuala in the morning on *An Lár* and we walked to the convent together. She sat a few rows behind me in the classroom but the only notes she wrote were to Sam which were in Irish. She also wrote letters to the newspapers about boycotting British goods as a protest against the things that were happening in the North.

I wondered if Dad knew about Sam's love of the Irish language, so when he was back in Drumbron for a few days I said to him, "Dad, Sammy writes in Irish to Nuala."

"Good for him."

"He said he's going to the Gaeltacht next year."

"It's only normal, he wants to be with Nuala."

"How did you know Sam was in love with Nuala?" and then realised he was Garda and knew everything that went on in town.

"Galway girls are special."

"Like Mammy? Will a Cavan boy fall for me like you fell for Mammy?

"Lassie, lads from all over the country will be falling for you like autumn leaves."

"So I will be able to have the big wedding Mammy wanted, instead of getting married at the side of the chapel?"

"Aye, you'll…"

Mammy came into the kitchen saying, "Mary, hurry up and finish your tea or you'll be late for study."

Dad and I stopped talking about the wedding Mammy never had.

The Facts of Life

In fifth year, we were considered young ladies and deemed old enough to be taught about the facts of life. At the beginning of November, the Catechism nun told us that we would have the honour of a visit from the Reverent Mother, who would give us the lecture. I told Evelyn.

"That auld witch in black is going to tell us about the birds and the bees!"

"No, it has nothing to do with nature. It's a lecture to prepare us for life."

"By a woman who never stepped outside the convent since she went into it? This is going to be hilarious."

"So, you are coming?"

"Wouldn't miss it for the world. Ricky can go to the races by himself and watch the horse he says is going to win, lose."

On the morning of the lecture there was a buzz of excitement as the sliding panels that divided the two classrooms were pulled back. A-class and B-class became one.

The Reverend Mother swept into the room with Sr Beatriz trailing behind, holding a long rolled-up canvass under her arm. All heads followed them as they headed for the top of the room and stepped onto the podium. A glance from the superior's eyes bade us to be silent while Sr Beatriz unrolled the tube to reveal a picture of Our Lady. She hung it on the board. We saw the Virgin Mary kneeling to the side of the Archangel Gabriel, her soft hands clasped in front of her, her eyes modestly cast down. A cough and a long ruler striking the desk made sure the few girls who weren't engrossed in the picture directed their eyes towards the young mother-to-be.

Ev nudged me but I was afraid to look at her because giggling hiccups were making my body shake. She whispered, "Is the Archangel a man or a woman, I wonder? With the dress and hair, it's hard to tell."

I stared intensely at the ruler as it tapped on the picture. My eyes following its swaying movement, hoping it would hypnotise me, put me in a trance and keep the laughter locked inside as the nun was saying, "Mary was a girl of fifteen when the angel appeared onto her. You girls are fifteen and sixteen, the same age as Mary when the angel appeared unto her, so it is proper and fitting…"

Ev whispered into my ear, "that I appear unto ye."

"…that you girls, who are the same age as Our Lady, should be as she was…"

"…with child," Ev said in my ear.

"When the angel told Our Lady she was with child, she wasn't surprised because, even though she was only fifteen, she knew women have babies."

"She'd be a right eejit if she thought men had babies," Ev whispered.

"When the angel announced onto her that she was with child, Mary answered 'I know not man.'…"

"She doesn't know what's she missing."

"…so we can see Our Lady knew a mother needed a father to have a child. For this reason, you girls who are the same age as Mary, should be like her."

"Having angels in my room, no way!" Ev said.

"…To be with child a girl has to know a man. When you girls leave school, you will meet young men who will want to walk out with you. Bear in mind that it is very important to behave like a young lady. When you see the young man you are walking out with is interested in marrying you, you may let him hold your hand, but you must never do so until he has asked for it in marriage."

"A hand? Is that all he gets?"

"…It is important to behave like a young lady and only give your gloved hand when you become engaged."

Ev continued commenting, "Ricky is behaving like a young gentleman, he hasn't held my hand yet as his two hands are always busy fumbling under my bra."

The laugh was lying low in my stomach, and I was doing a great job of keeping down but when the Reverend Mother repeated, "…Mary knew not man," Ev whispered, "And Mr Delaney's cows know not bull."

Giggling waves rippled across my belly sending sprays of titters spurting upwards as I remembered Mr Delaney sitting in our sitting room, with his lump of ham hands placed on his knees, the wispy hair racked across his shiny head, telling Mammy out of his tight, button size mouth how he was getting rid of his bull as he was going to have all his cows inseminated artificially.

"That bull had it too good for too long. Any cow he wanted, he could have had. But I'll put paid to his merriment. When he sees the vet doing what he used to do, he won't be parading around so high and mighty."

"John, you need to be careful. Bulls can be spiteful."

"Don't worry, Dervla, that bull is no match for me."

Remembering Mr Delaney comparing himself to the bull made me shake with laughter. I put my fist in front of my lips and coughed loudly to disguise the chuckles that rocked my body. Ev stood up and mouthed to Sr Beatriz, "Will I take Mary out to have a drink of water?" while she pointed to my body doubled up over the desk shaking with pent-up laughter, which I hope fooled the nuns into thinking it was a bout of coughing.

As soon as the nun nodded her head, Ev pulled my jumper, yanking me up and dragged me from the desk. We left the classroom and ran down the stairs while the Reverend Mother was warning the girls not to give their un-gloved hand to their fiancées. The touching of bare flesh against bare flesh could be 'an occasion of sin' for the boy. The girl would be responsible and have to go to confession as she may have caused the boy to sin in thought or deed.

Outside in the yard, Ev said, "What a load of rubbish! I let Ricky touch my diddies because I love the feeling."

"What feeling?"

"They tingle and the nipples go hard."

"Ev, you can't let him do that. It's a sin, I think."

"So Ar, un-bra-ed is the same or worse than un-gloved?"

"I'm sure it might be."

"You haven't a clue, so shut up."

"Confess anyway, to be on the safe side."

"I won't."

"You have to, it could be a mortal sin."

"Mortal sin is intercourse and the only course me and Ricky have is after-course."

"What do you mean, Ev?"

"After-course! Dessert! You know when Ricky buys me an ice cream after our bag of chips."

"But touching your diddies might be a sin. Ask the priest."

"No way. What business is it to the priest what I do with Ricky? If the priest wants to be entertained, let him read a book."

I wasn't convinced and was about to say something, but Ev didn't want to hear. She changed the subject straight away. "How's your mother? Mammy said she is still distraught about Jackie marrying that fellow last October. Sure, aren't we all distraught trying to pronounce that name Onassis, with how easy it was to say Kennedy."

Jackie Kennedy was Mammy's life. Her dearest wish was to meet the American ex-First Lady and Mouth was doing his best to help her.

"John, if William became President of Ireland, I'd meet Jackie, wouldn't I?"

"William, President of Ireland!" spluttered Mr Delaney, crumbs of cake spitting from his mouth.

"Yes. I would be the Irish President's wife and I would meet Jackie on her next visit to Ireland."

"That hat William wears would go against him being President," he said scraping the crumbs from his trouser legs.

"I'll make him wear him a different one."

"I don't know, did you ever see a young president? They're all old like De Valera."

"So will I never meet Jackie?" she mournfully asked the crumb-spitter.

"You will."

"How can you be so sure, John?"

"Because you'll meet her in heaven. She's a Catholic, so she's going up not down."

"John, how right you are! There's always heaven.

"You can become her friend in heaven."

"But John, we have to sure we get to heaven too."

"Of course we are going heaven. St Peter only let people like us in.

"But we have to make sure. That fat pope could have changed the rules for getting into heaven."

"To be on the safe side, we'll make the First Fridays."

"Why?"

"Because if you make the First Fridays, you are guaranteed a place in heaven. My mother makes them."

That was the reason Mammy and Mr Delaney went to Mass and communion on the first Friday of every month for nine months. To make sure they got into heaven, Mammy and Mr Delaney made about ninety First Fridays.

While they were making the nine Fridays, Jackie was getting excommunicated for marrying Onassis, causing Mammy no amount of anguish. She worried where Jackie would go when she died. Mr Delaney tried to comfort her suggesting different things they could do to make sure Jackie got into heaven.

"We could light a candle for her."

"I've lit enough candles to burn a house down and my prayers were never answered."

I remembered the time when I was small, and she prayed in front of the statue of Our Lady. I wondered what it was she had prayed for then.

"Dervla, you know how people pray for the conversion of Russia, well you and I could pray for the conversion of Jackie Kennedy."

"John, she is converted already. Sure, wasn't her mother an Irish-American Catholic and her father a French Catholic, so she can't be converted."

Ev, who was with me in the kitchen while they were talking, patted her lap, so I knew she was thinking of sending Miss Price-Hyde after Jackie, the lapsed Catholic.

"I never thought of that, Dervla."

"I know John, I always have to do the thinking for you."

"Well, how about having a Mass said for her?"

"The priest would say it on a weekday, and we'd have to go."

"What's wrong with that?"

"No one who is anyone goes to Mass during the week."

"My mother does."

"She's different, but you know what I mean about the people who go to Mass on the weekdays. I see very few stylish people at the First Fridays."

"How about making a novena?"

"That's so boring, John. Saying the same set of prayers for nine days."

"We could go to Knock for the nine days?"

"Knock is a one street town in the middle of a windy nowhere, John."

"Very windy. You'd wonder why Our Lady went to such a wild place. She had more sense when she went to Lourdes." Mouth paused for a moment as an idea struck him. "Maybe that's where we'll go," he said, and Mammy nodded her head in agreement.

"Lourdes wouldn't be bad. At least we'd get some sun and I'd see what kind of clothes the French wear. John, isn't it strange that Our Lady of Lourdes dressed the same as Our Lady of Knock?"

"She might be like a nun. They wear the same clothes always."

"But they don't appear to people in grottos?"

"They can't, they are not let out of the convent." They were having coffee, which must have had led Mr Delaney to say, "Lourdes is French, so the coffee must be good like the Italian. I wonder are there any little outdoor cafes like in Rome?"

"If the weather is anything like the weather in Mayo, I will not be having my coffee outdoors. I could do with a bit of sun, John, and so could you. What is the best time to go?"

"Dervla, we'll wait until after St Patrick's Day before we go to Lourdes."

"You're right, we'll be guaranteed the sun in April."

"I was thinking of the St Patrick's Day Parade and my new tractor. If we don't go til April, I'll be able to show it off."

"You are so lucky John with only having a tractor to think about. Here I am having to worry about what I'm going to wear to that GAA Dinner Dance that William takes me to every year. And on top of that, I have to buy the turkey and prepare our Christmas dinner."

"I will pick the dress for the GAA dinner, Dervla."

"I was counting on that, John."

Having decided to go to Lourdes, during the following weeks their conversations returned to what they had always been with Mouth informing us of the next festival or season expected. "When Christmas is over, we'll never feel 'til Easter is on us."

"When is Easter this year?"

"The end of March this year. We'll have time enough in the New Year to prepare for the trip."

"I'm glad to hear you say that, John, because that Nuala

McCabe, from the council house, is talking to Sammy about our trip as though we were going tomorrow."

"How does she know about our trip?"

"Sam and then there's Mary who tells her things too," my mother said, her eyes turned sideways towards me.

"What is she saying about our trip?"

"Wondering if we'll call into Samuel Beckett to congratulate him on winning a prize."

Samuel Beckett had won the Nobel Prize for Literature in October. Nuala and Sam were as thrilled as though they had won it themselves. While Nuala was showing us the paper with the Nobel Prize winner, Ricky was staring at the photo and said, "I know that fellow. What pub does he drink in?"

"Ricky, last year he was looking at you from the wall," my cousin Sam said.

"What was he doing on the wall?"

"He was in a framed picture. Samuel Beckett is an ex-pupil of the school you went to."

"No way? And now this guy from one of my schools is on the paper?"

"The school was Pretoria in Enniskillen."

"Enniskillen, was it? I'm sure glad I got out of that place. The feicing town is full of British soldiers. Anywhere you go, you see them with their guns."

"What were you doing in Enniskillen? Going back to see if your whiskey under the bed was safe?" Sam asked him, not sounding like Sam at all.

"I wanted to have a drink with a few fellas I met last year."

"If you are thinking of making friends with the soldiers, remember they only drink Scotch."

I laughed surprised at Sam. Maybe he wasn't as dry as we thought and more like Nuala who was full of ideas. She 'took the bull by the horns' as she used to say when wanted to do something. That was the reason she wasted no time in speaking to Fr Mannion about staging *Waiting for Godot* in the youth club.

"Father, as Christmas is coming, we were thinking you might like us to put on a play in the youth club."

"It's the further thing from my mind."

"But Father, wouldn't it be nice to have a Christmas play?"

"Like we had last year, you mean? When ye talked me into letting them do a live crib on *An Lár*." Nuala had convinced the priest to let us have people dressed like those who visited the stable when the Baby Jesus was born. She even got a loan of the cow and donkey from a farmer.

"Sure the baby in the manger never stopped bawling. The poor thing had the life frightened out of it with the ass braying and the sheep bleating!"

"Everyone liked it, Father."

"Indeed they did. They had a great laugh at the Three Wise Men looking stupid."

"Father, in *Waiting For Godot*, there are only two actors on the stage."

"I said I want no plays, not even one called *Waiting for the Three Wise Men*."

As Nuala couldn't stage *Waiting For Godot*, she decided to do a Christmas Quiz based on Beckett's work. She told me and Úna about it one of the frosty evenings we went sliding on Clonthu Hill.

First Love

When nights were crisp, the stars beamed in a navy-blue sky and the words from your mouth came out steamy, it meant the following day the grass and hedges would be dressed in shimmery, silvery frost, while a shiny, glittery scarf would cover roads decorated with diamonds of different sizes and shapes. Glassy pools awaited morning and the feet of children to crack them into spiderweb designs while we waited for the water thrown on Clonthu Hill to become a frozen stream.

For years, I went sliding on Clonthu Hill with Kait and Úna. It was mostly the kids from the council houses around the railway station that used the hill for sliding on the dark, freezing-cold evenings of winter.

I left the house as usual for Second Study that started at eight and finished at nine o'clock. Instead of going, I met up with Úna and Nuala at the far end of Kilmartin Road and we hurried up the hill. The previous night the lads had thrown buckets of water to create an icy path in the middle of the road.

I wasn't surprised to see Michael Stiff Neck's long, strong legs among the sliders who queued up on the flat crown of the hill. The first in line ran, gathering speed before lurching down onto their haunches at the head of the slide. Then they whizzed down on the frozen, glassy path to the bottom where they straightened their bodies and walked up the hill for another go.

What surprised me was the jerk in my chest when I saw Michael's hands go round the waist of Catherine McLoughlin, the person in front of him. She was looking back, smiling up at him. My fingers wanted to reach out and touch one of the wisps of hair that curled on his neck. Úna, catching my hand and pulling me up to top of the hill to get in line so we could slide, made me look away.

Michael was already at the bottom of the hill and had started coming back up the hill to join the line again when he saw me. He smiled. I felt my lips swell and tingle. I tried to smile back. Then he was standing at my side saying to Úna.

"I'm glad you kept the place for me," and stepped in behind me in the line. His face touched mine as he leaned forward to say, "Didn't know you liked sliding."

My whole body took on a soft glow. My mouth and throat turned marshmallow-y. I only could nod. When we ducked down onto our haunches, at the head of the slide, and I felt his hands on my waist, my body trembled. I wondered if the boy I was holding in front of me could feel the shake in my hands.

I was so wobbly when I got to the bottom that I fell flat on my bottom instead of popping up like I always did. Michael was still on his haunches, and he lifted himself and me up with no effort. Úna had straightened up and was on her way up the hill to the line again.

Michael was holding me from behind, leaning his head forward towards my ear asking me if I was alright. I turned around and my eyes looked up into his clear blue ones. I lowered them straight away because it was too much to look at him. My lips were shooting out of my face wanting to touch his when Kevin, the lad from the river, shouted, "Arlene didn't hurt herself. Michael move, so we get up the hill and back into line." That brought me back to earth but wrapped in a dreamy feeling of floating.

We walked back to the top of the hill trying not to look at each other. He made sure he was the one right behind me on the slide holding onto my waist. Each time we slid to the bottom, I leaned my body back against his and he lifted me up by the waist and turned me around to face him before we climbed back up the start of the slide. No one must have noticed we kept together because after a while when Úna got tired and went to sit on the wall of the Nun's Field, she called us and another few over to talk.

"Hey, did any one ye else hear about the bones found in the Home grounds?" Úna asked.

"Yeah, my brother said they were thousands of heads with hair and eyes."

"There wasn't any hair or eyes, it was only a few bones scattered around a concrete slab."

"Who put them there?"

"Maybe it was just a dog trying to hide his bones and he didn't root deep enough."

"Evelyn Curry told me her father, the garda, said they were bones from the people who died during the Famine," Úna said, like someone who knew what she was talking about. When the Irish were dying on the side of the road with green juice coming from their mouths, the people called what was happening '*An Ár Mór.*' It means 'The Great Slaughter' but with time it was softened to take the bite out of it and became known as 'The Famine.' Nan and Nanny had told us how whole villages died during this terrible time and the bodies were not buried because there was no one alive to bury them. By now, most of the sliders were gathered around talking about the discovery of the bones. Me and Michael let ourselves be pushed to the back of the crowd.

"If they were from the Famine there would be all sizes of heads, but everyone is saying the skulls were small, so they must be from children," Kevin said.

"For your information children died during the famine too," Úna's sister Teresa said.

"I know they did, my grandmother told me about them dying on the side of the road with their mouths green from eating the grass," Kevin answered back but he smiled at Teresa because he remembered her being a baby in the pram.

"Shut up you two," Úna ordered. "Does anyone know who found the bones?"

"I think it was a woman who lives near the Home."

"It wasn't, it was…" While Úna and the rest were talking and arguing about the bones, me and Michael were stepping sideways away from them.

It was dark, I stumbled on a stone I didn't see. Michael put out his hand to steady me. I held it and leaned the side of my body against his as we limped to the back of Nan and Nanny's old cottages where we were out of sight.

My mouth was full of tickles. I couldn't speak, so I looked up into Michael's face. His mouth opened as though he was about to speak. My lips took charge. They ascended towards Michael's. He lowered his. They brushed my lips lightly making my mouth tingle. My lips pressed themselves into the soft full ones of his mouth.

My body wanted to be closer to his. I stood on my tiptoes to bring it up higher. My arms wrapped themselves around his neck. He held me lightly against his body while mine was following the example of my mouth, melting into his chest. Immersed in this mist of wonderous sensations, I floated into oblivion. A cracking noise like a pebble hitting a window brought me and Michael out of our dreamy haze.

We pulled apart.

Sounds of stones hitting metal and feet running came from the other side of the houses. An image of the British soldiers with their guns flashed through my mind but the soldiers were in Derry, not on Clonthu Hill.

"Who's throwing stones?" Michael asked in a loud voice as we hurried out from the behind the house and saw lads flinging stones after a Morris Minor that sped away.

"What's happening?"

"The dirty old man was prowling around again."

"What dirty old man?"

"The one that's always offering lifts to young lads."

"But why are ye throwing stones at him?"

"Because we heard he likes the lads to touch him in certain parts."

"Who said that?" Nuala asked.

"Paddy O'Neill's brother Jack. Paddy told us that weird fellow showed his brother dirty magazines he had in the car."

"But Jack isn't small." Nuala knew his sister Pauline O'Neill.

"He is, only twelve."

"Why did he look at the magazines?"

"Your man had chocolate and cigarettes, so Jack thought he might as well get a few fags but when your man started touching his buddy, Jack got out of the car real fast."

Everyone went quiet. Then Úna said, "We have to tell the Gardaí about him. Do ye know who owns the car?"

"It's no good going, Úna. They'll do nothing."

"How do you know?"

"Cos Paddy's parents went but the Gardaí got annoyed with them for saying there was a man after boys. They said such things don't happen in Drumbron."

"Maybe if the pervert was on a bike, they might take notice but not of someone who owns a car," Nuala said.

"Well I'll tell my father and he'll do something. Did any of ye see the driver?" I asked.

"No one got a chance to see him. We were all over here near the wall."

"But who did he talk to?"

"To the few lads near the slide."

"Where did he come from?" I continued interrogating the boys, my father's daughter for sure.

"He appeared from the side of the auld houses there." And they pointed to Nanny and Nan's cottages. Me and Michael looked at each other wondering if the man had seen us.

"If Paddy hadn't spread the word, that filthy bugger could have coaxed one of the smaller lads into his car."

"So they didn't see his face."

"No, but luckily the two lads were cute enough to throw a stone at him and call him a dirty feicer, so he hopped it back into his car and drove off." Me and Michael were listening as people added bits about the prowler in the car, doing our best to look normal. Then Michael took part in the conversation asking Tom from the river, "Hey sham, did you ever see that Morris Minor around *An Lár*? Are ya wide to who owns it?"

"I swear to God, I never saw it in me life," said Tom, who was one of the corner boys famous for holding up the town hall wall. "Haven't a clue who owes that Morris Minor, sham. It doesn't be around town."

"He must be from out of town," Nuala said and added, "Hey Ar, it's half nine. We need to go."

"Yeah, you're right. We should just be about home from study now." I was in two minds about leaving. In one way I was glad at the chance of leaving because I was worried that I'd reach out and touch Michael's face but at the same time I didn't want to leave him.

Giving a quick glance to Michael I linked arms with Nuala and Úna. The three of us headed towards Kilmartin Road and along Sligo Road, talking about the bones and the dirty old man. We went up Railway Terence to the station so Úna and Nuala could go up the shortcut to their houses. Before she left us Nuala asked us to do some of the questions for the Beckett Quiz.

"Nuala, there isn't enough time before the Halloween Disco to prepare a pile of questions, so let's leave it for Christmas time," I told her, and she nodded her head.

Michael was the one I wanted to think about and not Beckett. I waited outside my house for about ten minutes hoping Michael had followed me, but he hadn't.

Lying in bed, I kept thinking about every second of the time we had spent together. I touched my lips with my finger remembering our kiss. The floating on air feeling was wonderful and at last I understood how Ev felt about Ricky and why Nuala wanted to be with Sam every minute of the time he was in Drumbron. I fell asleep dying for the following evening to come and to be on the slide again with Michael.

I didn't feel hungry the next morning, but Mammy made me eat a slice of toast. At school, Nuala was talking about the Halloween Disco. She assumed I'd be in the parish hall as usual helping her cut eyes in turnips and hang sheets, so they looked like ghosts, around the hall.

I wasn't interested in making scary decorations for everyone to enjoy except Michael who didn't go to the youth club. Itinerants knew without being told that they wouldn't be welcome, so they stayed away. An unwritten law kept the itinerants from playing football with the GAA as well. People assumed they were better with their fists than with their feet – boxing was their thing.

If Michael was at the boxing club, I could see him, so on my way to First Study, I walked past the building where the itinerants trained for their boxing matches. The coach was an Englishman who had met and married a Drumbron girl in London. When he started the club, there was talk about letting girls train, but Fr Mannion was set against the idea of girls boxing. I didn't even know if Michael was into boxing, but it was the only place where the teenage Travellers hung out. I didn't see him even though I walked up and down in front of the building for half an hour.

The Bones in the Home

When I went home for tea after First Study, Mr Delaney was in the kitchen talking about the bones. According to him the bones were of the Famine victims.

"I was there this morning with the priest."

"Aren't you good, John. Were there many more people around?"

"Just myself, the priest and two or three others. We said a few prayers for the souls of the departed and the priest blessed the spot."

"So he splashed a drop of holy water around the place," I said and got a vexed look from Mammy.

"Mary! There weren't many bones, were there, John?"

"I wouldn't say so, Dervla. The county council workers put a bit of cement around the slab, so there no danger of anyone else falling into the manhole underneath it."

"What were the children up to playing there. It shouldn't be allowed."

"Exactly what I said myself. And besides, there are those slides. I spoke to the county council workers telling them I wouldn't be doing their work anymore."

"What work would that be now that you are doing, John?"

"This morning I poured a bag of salt over the slide on Tinker Hill. I told the workers I want them to make sure there are no slides anywhere else in town."

As I listened to what they were saying, I felt myself getting angry. What right had this self-righteous, baldly man to decide what the young people of Drumbron could and couldn't do.

"I'm glad someone has some sense in their heads, John. Mrs Fitzgerald told me her serving girl Mary hurt her leg on that slide last winter and was off work for a few hours the next morning, so it's about time someone put a stop to that dangerous carry on."

"I'm tired of telling Fr Mannion you can't have youngsters out at night. God knows what they get up in the dark."

I lowered my head and remembered Michael's lips.

"I'll put a stop to the gallivanting that goes on up there. Tomorrow night at the council meeting, I'm putting forward a motion calling on the council workers to spread salt on any slide they see."

"What a great idea, John. When Mary was small, she wanted to pour water on the lane outside the house but there was no way I'd have a bunch of children screaming outside my gate."

"If that was all they got up to, Dervla, we'd be alright. You wouldn't believe the things I hear that goes on in the dark." He was looking at me as he said it and I wondered if he knew about me and Michael. "I have to talk to Garda Curry about a certain lad."

"Who would that be now, John."

"You wouldn't know him, Dervla, but his father is known to the Gardaí, so like father, like son."

"What is the blackguard doing?"

"Filthy stuff altogether. I won't soil your ears with the details but Dervla, I'll just say the girl is as willing as him to commit the sin of impurity." He told Mammy whose eyes had lit up because these were the conversations she loved.

"John, would I know the girl he is leading astray?"

"Enough to say the girl is from a respectful family and it

would break her mother's heart if she had to spend time with an aunt in England."

He was glancing over at me as he said this. I hated him and wanted to take a run and jump at his fat, ugly face and rub my hand through the stupid stripes of hair plastered on his head. I stood up with such fury that the chair fell back.

"Mary, what's got into you? Would you mind getting up quietly like a young lady does."

"I can't help it if the chair fell. Look, I'm picking it up," I glared at her, forgetting I had to be careful.

"A change of school where they'd teach you manners might do you good."

Straight away I changed tactics and addressed her in a milder tone. "Mammy, I'm upset because the bones that were found in the Home could be of someone who was murdered."

"Murdered!"

"In the pictures when they find bones there is always a killer on the loose in the town, so maybe there is a murderer in Drumbron."

She put her hands on her chest and said crossly, "Oh for God's sake Mary, how could you ever think such a thing? This is Ireland, not pagan England. You are living among decent people, so get those ideas out of your head this minute." She turned to Mouth and said, "John, you were saying there does be queer goings on with certain youngsters?"

"And Dervla, I can assure you that certain boy I was talking about will be taking the boat to England tonight if he or his father doesn't want to see the inside of Mountjoy Jail."

I wanted to charge at the stupid man but had to go through the motions of not knowing what he was talking about, so I said, "Mammy, I'm off to Late Study now."

"Isn't it a bit early?"

"It is but Nuala wants me to give her a hand with Halloween Disco, so if ye don't mind, I'm off now."

I left and walked to where the boxing club was on the little lane near the pitch. There was no one about. I waited a while, but no one appeared so I headed up to the convent. Úna was at the gate.

"Ar, terrible news. The council workers are putting salt any slide they see. They told Paddy O'Neill the Gardaí will be watching in the evening in case any of the lads throw water on the road."

"It's not fair. There nothing we can do in winter except slide."

Then she came out with something that left me flabbergasted. "Michael McDonagh is gone to England."

"He can't be, I saw him last night."

"I did too but he's went to Dublin this evening."

"Are you sure?"

"Why would I say it if it wasn't true? Paddy O'Neill told me Michael left so the Gardaí wouldn't torment his father. They are trying to put the blame on him for a house that was broken into."

"What house? I didn't hear anything about a break-in?"

"One in Kilmartin Road that's vacant for months and sure you wouldn't mind but there's nothing in it to steal."

"But the Gardaí must know well Michael had nothing to do with break-in. He's good."

"Of course they know but they want to get rid of Michael for some reason or other."

"They can't do that."

"They can, Garda Curry drove Michael to the Holyhead boat."

"He didn't!"

"He did and even bought him the ticket."

"Why would he do that?"

"To make sure Michael got on the boat."

"God. That's madness."

"Yeah, but you can be sure the Garda told Michael not to come back if he knew what was good for him."

I wanted to hear every detail of what had happened, so I skipped Study and went with Úna up to her house. As usual, a relative from Derry was in the kitchen talking to Mr McNulty. Úna and I crossed over to the graveyard to get away from the stupid relative.

"Why did Garda Curry made Michael go on the boat to England?"

"That's what the Gardaí do when they want to get rid of someone."

"My father is a Garda. He wouldn't do such a thing, Úna."

"Sure I know your father wouldn't, but some Gardaí don't like the itinerants."

"Because there's fights at their funerals," I said remembering how Dad used to talk about the trouble at such-and-such a tinker's funeral when I was small.

"We all know that, but some Gardaí are mean. My father said he got awful beatings when he was in the Curragh."

"That's not true. My father wouldn't ever hit anyone, so shut up saying things like that."

"I'm just saying what my father said. Maybe it was the soldiers who beat them up and not the Gardaí. Don't get mad. Sorry," she said trying to make up.

But I was upset and ready to be angry and said, "I don't

criticise your father. You should think before you talk." I walked off in a huff.

She called after me, "If I hear anything else about Michael, I'll let you know."

I was annoyed with Úna. All I wanted to do was to talk about Michael, to tell her how I remembered his kiss, his lips drawing mine to his, my mouth touching the soft warmth, the feeling of wanting to melt into him as my mind floated away. I wanted to share the memories of our kiss, to savour every second of the magic moment but Úna ruined it by telling me Michael had been sent away. I was angry with Úna until much later that night when, like a raindrop starting to roll from the leaf in a tree, it hit me it was Mr Delaney's fault that I might never get another kiss from Michael. So a few days after my sorta-row with Úna when she said the Gardaí were mean, we were friends again.

Inquisitor. Tomás de Torquemada – Delaney

Mr Delaney was a right eejit and yet certain things were done because he said so. The stupid man took it on himself to be the guardian of people's behaviour and to make sure there would be no 'occasions of sin' around Drumbron. He had the authority to get council workers to destroy the slides – about the only places we had fun for free on winter evenings.

At school we were learning about the Inquisition. I don't know what the Spanish inquisitor, Tomás de Torquemada, looked like but I imaged him as ugly and smug as Mouth Delaney. The Inquisition, in sunny Spain with cities like Granada and Kings who could build Armadas, controlled people's lives. Mouth Delaney – in our dreary, wet town, had as much power over people as the Inquisition had in Spain. He decided if kids from the council estates were allowed to slide or if Michael could kiss a girl like me.

The Inquisition had agents and spies all over Spain looking for heretics. Mouth Delaney must have had spies in Drumbron too. He knew about any girl that got into trouble. He and Mammy used to say the girls' sins showing up as a baby served them right for being weak and wanton.

A man like Mr Delaney decided how people lived because the Delaney's had land, money and businesses. They were the 'Big People' of Drumbron. At every election people voted for him as a town councillor and put the fate of the town and its people into his hands. Their reasoning being if the Delaneys had prospered, then any member of the clan would know what was good for the town. This ignorant man was treated with the near-tugging of the forelock. The only tugging I wanted to do to him was to scratch the look of certainty that glinted from little piggy eyes in his fat, greasy face, scream at him, kick his shins and ask him what harm was there in living and being happy, but I didn't.

I was afraid of Mammy and the power she had of being able to send me off to be locked up in a laundry. My fear made me keep quiet. I couldn't confront my mother openly even though my body screamed in pain. My throat was sore holding down the thoughts I couldn't let out in words. My jaw ached with the grinding of my teeth inside my clenched mouth. My pounding head weighed heavily on my neck, stiffening it rigid. Four marks were carved into my palms as my nails dug deep into the flesh.

Every time I saw Mr Delaney in my house with his gob full of Chester cake, I wanted to scream and ask why a dirty old man was free to frighten young boys and why bones from a person were thrown back under the concrete slab as though they belonged to a dog, but I didn't. I went upstairs and shed tears. Outside the trees were doing the same, covering the ground with streaks of russet and gold. The bleak days hid under the cover of darkness, leaving long evenings where Michael and our kiss was all I had.

My birthday came. I was sweet sixteen but felt dead inside. I went through the motions of celebrating this day that was as empty as the others.

Úna gave me a gift box of talcum and body cream from the chemist. Nuala and Sam gave me a book by Samuel Beckett. I smiled but knew I would never look at it.

Ev invited me to *Hello Dolly* in the Odeon. Ricky wouldn't come. He didn't trust our opinions on what pictures to see because after we went to *Midnight Cowboy*, he came out bucking mad saying there were no cowboys or Indians in it.

I loved the film and cried with the sadness of life the film portrayed and because Jon Voight could have been Michael if the lips were thinner, and he had nicer eyes.

The day after my birthday I got a birthday card from Kait. I didn't feel like reading the letter inside it, but I did because 'that's why,' as Kait herself would say. At the end of it she asked me if I had been to see Mrs Lynch. I hadn't even thought about the woman who never went outside the door, so I went to Delia's to see if she knew where the woman lived.

Maggie opened the door and spoke which was surprising. "Come in or that, it will do Delia good to see you."

"Is she alright?"

"Them bones are bringing back memories and keeping us from sleeping."

"Is she upset because of the bones?"

"Indeed we are."

I realised I was being ignorant excluding Maggie as though she didn't count, so I touched her on the arm, but she withdrew it real quick saying, "The not wanting to remember, going through her mind, is what's going through mine too."

"It's hard, no right burial."

"But it was us who did what the nuns told us to do. We did it with heavy hearts, but we did it."

Delia's voice came from the kitchen. "Is that yourself, Arlene, coming to see us? Did you bring your Aran jumper?"

"I finished it, Delia, and it was thanks to you that half the stiches didn't drop to the floor but stayed on the needles." When I got to the kitchen, Delia was sitting by the fire with two dogs on each side, another in front and a cat on her lap.

"How are you, Delia? I'm surprised you don't have a cat on your head too."

"Aren't you the cheeky girl!" She gave a quick smile and said, "I'm not the best, a grá. I'm thinking of the little babies. They won't leave my head."

I wasn't used to seeing her sad, so I said the first thing that came to my head. "What babies, Delia?"

"The ones from the Home. Aye, the poor little babies."

"I knew two Home Babies, Liam and Brigid. Did you know them?"

"Every second girl was called Brigid but there wasn't that many Liams. Would you know anything else about them?"

"I wouldn't. Me and Kait used to sit beside them at school.

Look, she sent me a birthday card," I said showing her it. "She wants me to go and see the woman with the bad legs who swam back from the Titanic. Do you know where she lives?"

"Would it be Mrs Lynch you're wanting?"

"That's the name Kait told me."

"I was going there myself to see her this evening, but sure it'll do me no harm to leave the house now."

"Grand, cos I don't know her."

"The poor creature never goes outside the door. She'll be glad of a visit especially at this time of the year."

"Ducking Night you mean?"

"The lonely, long evenings. I mean when you have time to think. Hand me that packets of fig rolls for her." I picked up the packet of biscuits from the table.

"Maggie, take the face off you. Isn't there Kimberly biscuits in the press that you can stuff your mouth with when we're gone." The cats didn't like being put down, but the dogs were delighted with the idea of a walk, so we left with three dogs trailing behind.

Mrs Lynch lived in number fifteen, a few houses up from Delia's so there wasn't much time to ask about the mysterious woman from the Titanic.

"Why doesn't Mrs Lynch leave her house?"

"She finds it hard to walk."

"On account of her legs getting frozen when she swam back from the Titanic?"

"Where did you hear that? The poor woman was very sick after giving birth to her daughter and…"

Delia didn't finish the sentence because we were at the door, and she knocked on it. We hear a chair moving and the heavy breathing of a person and then someone shuffling down the hall towards the door. It opened and a woman with a fresh face stood in the frame. She was gasping and heaving. The effort of walking down the hall had left her without breath in her body.

"I hope we're not disturbing you now, Kathleen?"

"Indeedin, ye are not. Amn't I always happy to see a face and especially yours, Delia. And who would this beautiful girl be now?"

"Superintendent Blake's daught…" Before Delia had finished there was loud bang. The cross-door had slammed.

"I have the window open and sure with the way the wind is blowing, it's no wonder the door banged shut," she said as she hobbled down the hall. When she got to the door, she tried to open it, but she didn't have the strength to turn the knob.

"Let me do that for you, Kathleen, *a grá*."

"That's good of you, Delia. Will ye have a cup of tea?"

"We won't say no. I'll fill the kettle and put it on the range, so you sit and talk to Arlene, who as I was saying is the daughter of Superintendent Blake or maybe he's got an even higher job now. Isn't that right, Arlene?"

"Daddy is a Detective Chief Superintendent now, I think."

"So Kathleen, as you can hear, Arlene's father is in the Special Branch."

"I don't know what branch he's in, just that he goes to Dublin a lot."

"I had my baby in a hospital in Dublin but that was more than twenty years ago. It's very good of you to come with Delia to see me, Arlene."

"Mrs Lynch, Kait Kenny is my friend. Look this is the beautiful birthday card she sent me."

"She's a great girl so she is. A week doesn't go by that I don't get a letter from Kait telling me everything about her new life in that hospital with the nuns."

I felt a pang of jealousy. Then my mind told me Kait was kind-hearted. It was only normal she wrote to this housebound woman. I realised I was very selfish begrudging Mrs Lynch a letter from Kait.

This half-crippled woman found it hard work just to go as far as the front door. I could walk and go out any time I liked but Mrs Lynch couldn't. When we were leaving, I realised I was smiling. Delia and Mrs Lynch had cheered me up.

After that first visit when I felt like lying on the bed staring at the ceiling and thinking of Michael, I forced myself to get up and go and see Mrs Lynch. I didn't offer to make the tea on the first day I went on my own. Then I saw what a big effort it was for her to lift up the kettle and pour the water into the teapot. After that I always made the tea talking like Delia. "Sit down there now and take the weight off your feet."

"Well, aren't you the great girl. I'd do it myself only the pain in my back does be killing me if I lift anything heavy."

While we were having the tea, she asked what I wanted to be when I did my Leaving. I told her I was going to Art College.

Mrs Lynch knew about Van Gough and Spanish painters like Goya. She said she understood Goya's 'black period' because there were times when she was down in the dumps too and knew if she painted, her pictures wouldn't be always bright sunflowers.

"Mrs Lynch, I have plenty of canvasses and paint brushes. Will I bring you some and sometimes we could paint together?"

The Art Studio

Her kitchen became an art studio. At first, we propped the canvasses against a bowl on the edge of the table that had an oilcloth draped on it, the points, like triangles, sticking out at the corners. When her husband Mr Lynch saw he couldn't put his plate on the table while we were painting, he fastened a sort of stand that his wife could sit in front of and use as an easel.

She liked to paint sitting down as the pains in her back got worse when she was standing. I was surprised at how good she was and also that I could share my secrets with her, and she didn't look at me as though I had two heads. One evening while she was splashing paint on a canvass, I told her about having a crush on Michael the Traveller boy.

"The Traveller men are a handsome breed, well-built and fit as fiddles."

"Michael is handsomer than Troy Donohue any day."

"Not going out stopped me from knowing who that Donahue lad is," she said so I told her he lived in Hollywood and promised to bring her a poster so she could how fab he was. Then I gave out about Nuala and her stupid quiz.

"Nuala keeps on to me about the Beckett Quiz, but I haven't thought of a single question to ask, Mrs Lynch."

"Beckett!! How could you be thinking of him when your mind is on that fine looking lad you told me about?"

"Is it normal, Mrs Lynch, to be always thinking of Michael?"

"I was the same about my Declan when I first knew him.

Now whenever *I'll take you home again Kathleen* comes on the radio, I remember how he told me he'd take me home from that hospital and everything would go back to normal."

"My mother used to be sick too when she had babies, Mrs Lynch."

"The poor woman."

"Dad used to carry the babies back to the sawmills. That's why I have no brothers or sisters."

"Your father is a good man like my Declan. It's not many men who would stick by an invalid wife like Declan has."

"Will you never get better?"

"If I didn't get better by now, there's little hope. So getting back to the quiz, what kind of questions would ye want because as I have nothing to do, I'll help you with it."

"About Beckett's life, where he was born, you know that sort of thing. Did you ever read anything by him?"

"I did, that book of short stories with the funny name."

"What one?

"*More Pricks than Kicks*."

"Mouth Delaney is a prick."

"Why do you call him Mouth?"

"We started calling him Chester Cake Mouth because he used to eat all my father's Chester cake and then it got shortened to Mouth."

She laughed and then quietly said, "Them Delaney's were always cute hoors."

I didn't know what to say to that, so I asked, "What else did you read from Beckett?"

"His novel *Murphy* and the play *Waiting for Godot*."

"You're great."

"Reading is all I've done for years. Any book I get my hands on I read."

"I didn't know."

"I finished *The Borstal Boy* by Brendan Behan and I never stopped laughing."

"I have piles of books at home I can give you."

"That would be great and maybe you could go the library and get me books like Kait used to do."

"Of course I will, Mrs Lynch."

The black cloud hoovering over my head became grey when I was in Mrs Lynch's kitchen painting and getting things off my chest, like my disgust at Mr Delaney.

"You know, Mrs Lynch, I hate that Mr Delaney more than anyone. It's his fault Michael had to leave Ireland. I'm so mad at him that I hope he dies roaring."

She laughed at that and much more when I imitated his tiresome, 'We'll never feel until Christmas is on us!' which I had to listen to every time he came to visit which was every day.

Christmas Time

Christmas was coming and the geese were getting fat, but Mammy wasn't putting any pennies in my hat, so I didn't know how I could buy a present for my lovely Mrs Lynch who I was getting very fond of and wishing to make her life a bit easier.

She found it hard to lift things up. Even the teapot shook in her hands. If I had money, I would have bought a flask, so Mr Lynch could make her tea and put it in the flask to keep warm for her to drink during the day when he was at work.

It was doing my head in wondering what I could get her. During these ponderings, a watch I never used kept looking at me until I realised it was telling me it was the perfect present for her.

Mrs Lynch had the habit of stopping when we were talking to listen to the planes flying overhead. She'd say that such-and-such plane was on its way to Shannon, so I thought if she had a watch she would know if the flights were late or on time.

It was great relief to know I had the present got for her, especially as she was so good and had written the twenty questions for the Beckett quiz as she had promised.

Quiz Night

The quiz was easy but that didn't stop everyone in the club complaining about it as they were dead set against anything scholarly or highbrow. "Why can't we have a Fancy-Dress Contest instead of this stupid quiz?" they whinged. Even Fr Mannion said a fancy dress would be better than asking questions about some Protestant who wrote ridiculous plays that no one understood.

As it was too late to organise a costume competition for Christmas, Nuala promised she would have a fancy-dress disco and competition ready for St Patrick's Day. Fr Mannion agreed on the condition we came dressed as saints, kings or objects that were in Ireland at the time of St Patrick.

GAA Dance

Daddy had arrived in early December, a while before the GAA Dinner Dance. I spent as much time as I could talking to him even though I wasn't the small girl I used to be.

"Arlene, I can't pick you up and swing you around as you are not a wee lass. Mammy tells me you got great marks this term."

"I did."

"What did you ask Santa for? I'm sure he'll bring it to you."

"I'll tell you later when I write my letter to Santa." I waited until Mammy was gone to get her hair done before I asked him if he would teach me to drive.

"If it wasn't dark, we'd go now but first thing tomorrow morning we'll go back the Suileen Lane, and I'll give you your first lesson."

"Daddy, you are the best daddy in the world!"

"Only in the world?"

It was great he was at home.

Driving Lessons

I sat in the driver seat and Dad talked me through the steps of turning the key and pressing my foot on the accelerator. The first few times the car jerked forward, but in no time I had the hang of it. He told me there was no need to grip the steering wheel so tight as I would only have to move it when I wanted to change the direction.

We drove slow in second gear at the beginning but once I knew how to brake smoothly, I drove faster along Suileen Lane. After a few lessons, I was driving home and parking the car outside our gate. Then Daddy frightened the wits out of me by saying when we are going out on Sligo Road.

"Arlene, you're ready to go on the main road."

"I can't, Dad. I might crash into the cars."

"You won't but there will always be other cars on the road. The most important thing is not to be frightened. When you are walking on the street you don't keep bumping into people, do you?

"No, of course not."

"On the road you are not going to bump into other cars either."

He was right. I didn't crash into anything.

While I was learning to drive, I didn't have as much time to think about Michael because at night I was busy going through the steps of putting the car in gear. I was also planning where I would take Kait when she came home for a holiday in summer.

Dad stayed until the New Year. Before he left with the car for Dublin, I drove as far as Mrs Lynch's house and beeped the horn a few times before I got out of the car. With a box of oil paints and some canvases under my arm, I knocked on her door. When she pulled the door open slowly, I dangled the keys in front of her face and said, "Look Mrs Lynch, I know how to drive."

"Aren't you the great girl."

"Maybe one day I can take you for a spin."

"Wouldn't that be wonderful altogether."

"Where's Fluffy?" I said as I went to the kitchen to leave down the things I had under my arm. Fluffy was the white kitten Delia had given her for Christmas.

"The little devil keeps going back to Delia's house to play with its brothers and sisters."

"I won't run over him, I promise."

"He's too cute to go on the road."

We spoke for a while and then I told her I was going. "Well, I'm off. See ya next week."

"Isn't it grand for some people," she said but was smiling and happy for me.

Mr Delaney had started with his usual rigmarole.

"There's a great stretch in the evenings. We'll never feel it until Lent is on us."

"You are right, John. Before we know it, we'll be off to Lourdes."

Preparing for the trip helped Mammy forget the Pope had excommunicated Jackie Kennedy and not Bernadette Devlin.

"John, can you understand a Pope excommunicating an elegant lady like the First Lady and let that disgusting, mini-skirted girl with the hair falling all over her face be part of the Church?"

"Dervla, popes don't understand women's fashion. You only have to look at the nuns to know that."

"You're right, John, but what it isn't right is that there's pictures of that young pup in the same magazine as Jackie."

I picked up the magazine and started looking at the photos of the young MP from Derry. She pulled it from my hand.

"This magazine will never enter my house again," she said but changed her mind when Mr Delaney said, "Dervla, you can be sure if the men who landed on the moon had to leave magazines there for the Martians to see, they would have left ones with photos of Jackie Kennedy and not that rebel with the megaphone."

"John, do you think so? I'll ask William but the truth is, I never saw him with a magazine in his hand. By the way, he told me that I will need a passport for Lourdes."

In Drumbron, Mr Delaney was considered the expert on foreign travel as he had been to Rome with his mother, so he told Mammy where to have her photograph taken and helped her filled out the passport forms. Being busy with getting the green little book with her photo and her physical description on the first page in English and Irish, kept her mind off Jackie. It even helped her to forget that Terry Wogan was leaving the Irish radio and going to the BBC.

The Trip to France

The travel agency in Sligo booked the plane seats and the hotels. Mr Delaney asked them about renting a car, so he and Mammy could drive to Paris.

Dad, who was back from Dublin for a few days, twitched when he heard this and said, "John, they drive on the right on the Continent. Dervla's nerves would be shattered if she saw cars going the wrong way."

"Don't I often drive the tractor on the wrong side of the field myself and there's nothing to it."

"I know, John but a field is not a road with cars coming towards you in the other direction. Besides, the road signs are in French so it's better you go by train to Paris."

"My mother knows French. She says *éclair* and *hor d'oeuvre* in a perfect French accent. And Dervla is learning how to ask for a needle and thread from that little phrase book she has, so we are ready for anything that comes our way."

"A lot of good an *éclair* will do if yis have a puncture. Take the train and forget about the car, John."

"Dervla is in safe hands with me at the wheel, William."

"John, if you drive, my wife is not going on the trip," Dad said in his Garda voice.

The talk about renting a car was dropped. The trip was scheduled for the first week of April so Mr Delaney's tractor could be in the parade.

The St Patrick's Day Parade

St Patrick's Day was cold with a fine drizzle, but it didn't stop people lining the streets to get a glance of the floats, lorries and bands that flowed through the town.

Miss Price-Hyde, one of the organisers, had decided the shiny, bright green Ferguson should go at the head of the parade, in front of the fire engine. That was the reason Mr Delaney's new tractor was in front with Mouth behind the wheel, going slower than he does in his car so as to show off its newness and splendour, and making everyone else trail behind it.

The parade was passing through *An Lár*, heading up Church Street, when Legless, who was in the crowd, took a notion into his head and leapt onto the fire engine. He started hooting the horn and set the alarm off, making the light on the roof flash, roaring he was going to burn the bishop's house down with the bishop inside it and no fire engine was going to put the fire out.

Two firemen tried to grab him. He pushed them away, jumped off and ran towards the green tractor, which was going so slow he had no trouble hopping onto it. Mr Delaney said in an angry tone, "What do you think you are doing dirtying my brand-new tractor with them filth wellingtons?"

Legless looked at Mr Delaney's hair and raised his hand as though to ruffle it while saying, "And what do you think you doing with a head on you like streaky bacon?"

He shoved Chester Cake Mouth off the seat, sat on it himself and put his two hands on the wheel. Mr Delaney touching his head and feeling his hair was safe in place, decided it was better to risk his life by jumping off than to stay near the madman who wanted to mess with his hair. Legless drove the tractor away from the line of moving vehicles and raced towards Castle Fields, knowing that The Bishops Palace was in that direction.

The Gardaí ran like madmen to get into the squad car and go after him. People left the parade and started following the Gardaí who were following Legless on the tractor. Legless was near the bridge, the one where we hung out with Jim Smith and Ricky after the Legion meetings. He kept looking behind to see if the Gardaí were catching up and didn't realise he was driving too near the river. Two wheels of the tractor left the solid ground and hung in the air for a second before the tractor plunged into the river, making such a big splash that shot water upwards.

"Legless can't swim!" shouted Tom of the town hall. Heads turned towards the river and even the sign of the cross was made by some of the women praying for Legless, thinking he was trapped underneath the tractor at the bottom of the water. Thanks to their prayers a miracle happened and at that very moment we saw Legless scrambling out the water.

He tried to run but the weight of his wet trousers and his wellingtons filled with weedy water made his legs go in slow motion. The Gardaí grabbed him and pushed him into the squad car. They didn't even take him to the barracks but drove straight to Ballinacora.

The whole town had left the parade and were down at the river watching the spectacle. While Legless was being driven off, the two tug-o-war teams from the parade united to rescue the tractor. A few of the men jumped into the river with their ropes coiled around their shoulders. Instructions were shouted down to them as to how to place the ropes around the vehicle. The tug of war ones on the bank then wrapped the ropes around their hands. Digging their heels in the earth, they pulled in unison. After a few tries and cheers from the crowd. "Ye have her lads!" the tractor was hauled out and stood on dry ground, greener than in the morning because of the amount of slime stuck to the sides.

Races and Hairstyles

Legless' race and Mr Delaney's streaky bacon hair style became the talk of the town.

The next day, Mouth bought a cap. When a drunk in town shouted after him, "Hey are you trying to keep the rasher on your head warm with that cap?" Mr Delaney asked Dad to get the Gardaí to caution the drunk. Dad was doing his best not to look at Mouth's head while Mammy was saying, "At least Legless didn't get near the bishop. It's bad enough we have that Bernadette Devlin wan disgracing the Irish people in the English Parliament, without having someone from our town attacking the bishop."

This piece of grovelling ignorance annoyed me, so I shouted angrily, "I'm glad Bernadette slapped that liar, Reginald Maudling, across the face. He deserved what he got. Pity she didn't let him have a few more wallops for not apologising for murdering the people in Derry."

My mother was too stupid to see that Bernadette was a great Irish warrior. Dad was glaring at me with a Garda-type look in his eye while drowning me out by saying in a crisp voice, "As least they managed to pull your tractor out of the river, John."

"It's not the same tractor, William. It will never be the right after the ordeal it suffered. I told Miss Price-Hyde it's a sad day when a tractor can be kidnapped in broad daylight by a madman. At the next town council meeting I intend to put forward a motion about issuing passes," said Mr Delaney.

"Issuing passes?" Dad asked with a puzzled look on his face.

"Yes, to screen the people we let in to view the parade."

"Legless is in a padded cell in Ballinacora and you can be sure he'll be there for the next few St Patrick Day parades. Don't waste the council's time bringing that issue up."

"John, as least we have something to thank Our Lady for when we go to Lourdes. Legless is locked up and William says he won't see the outside of Ballinacora for a long time," Mammy said to comfort Mr Delaney and his bacon head.

The St Patrick's Day Fancy Dress Disco

As she had promised at Christmas time, Nuala organised a fancy-dress competition for the St Patrick's Day Disco, asking members to come as saints or kings or objects that were around at the time of St Patrick. When Fr Mannion saw me and Nuala arrive before the doors opened, his eyes looked puzzled at the black cardboard cloud I had pinned on top of the big Spanish comb the Spanish women wear with their mantillas and asked, "What in God's name is that on your head? A beetle?"

"No, Father, it is the black cloud that hung over Deirdre of the Sorrow's head when she was exiled to Scotland."

"Are you saying that pagan woman was around at the time of St Patrick?"

"A bit before him."

"A bit before him! Don't know where you got that idea from. She had nothing but nothing to do with Christianity!"

"The people of Ireland were pagans when St Patrick came, so the Celtic culture was still on the island."

"Whether it was or wasn't, that costume is disqualified."

I identified with what had happened to Deirdre of the Sorrows. She was a beautiful baby. When the old King heard she would grow up to be the most beautiful woman in Ireland, lust made him want her as his wife. To keep the young men away, she was reared in the woods with only women around her.

Diarmuid, a man as handsome as my Michael, followed the deer he was hunting into that woods. Deirdre saw him and they fell madly in love. The High King didn't like it one little bit and the pair of lovers had to flee to Scotland. Like Deirdre, I had been in a town without seeing any boy I fancied until I fell in love with Michael. One of Delaney's men saw us. Michael was exiled and a cloud of sorrow hung over my head.

"Miss McCabe, as least you listen to me," the priest said because Nuala came as a monk holding a quail. When Sam turned up later, he was the manuscript.

Úna was St Bridget and Ev was a snake, dressed in a long, tight dress with a hood of the same green colour. There was disapproval all over Fr Mannion's face, but he didn't disqualify her or expel her like St Patrick had done with the snakes.

Ricky didn't come until it was nearly over, so Fr Mannion didn't see him with a bottle of whiskey, saying he was a well full of holy water. Jim Smith was with Ricky holding a steering wheel from a tractor in his hands and shamrocks plastered all over his head with brill cream, as though they were weeds from a river, saying he was Legless.

A few days after the parade and just before Mammy went to Lourdes, I heard her and Batt, the postman, talking in the kitchen. Mammy always gave Batt a cup tea to oil his mouth. He was like a twin of Mr Delaney, with the same shiny head and a mouth full of gossip.

"So, Batt, you heard them saying there's enough single women around Drumbron without John having to go off foreign with another man's wife."

"Dirty minds who have nothing better to do than talk about decent people."

"Well, let them know John's mother is coming with us and that will put a stop to their gossiping."

"Indeed I will. Did ya hear about that wan who is going around saying she's a chiropodist?"

"Who would that be now, Batt?"

"The young Kelly wan who's back from her aunt in Liverpool. She was there long enough to get thin and now she's going into men's houses cutting their toenails, *mar dhea*."

"It won't be long before she has to go to her aunt's house again if that's the way she is carrying on."

"You can say that again, Mrs Blake."

When I heard that piece of gossip was going around about Mammy and Mr Delaney, I was upset and spoke to Dad. "Daddy, will people be talking about Mammy when she goes to Lourdes with Mr Delaney?"

"Why would they? A few might begrudge she can go abroad."

"But she's going with Mr Delaney."

"And his mother. I heard Mrs Delaney had a Mass said for their safe journey. All her pals in the Mass and Communion brigade know her son is a pure, young man and that she is going with him to make sure he remains as pure as the driven snow."

"You really don't mind Mammy going places with Mr Delaney?"

"Arlene, Mammy is on her own a lot since I took up my new position. She has no sisters so it good for her to have John to talk to."

Kait sent me a card for St Patrick's day. I wrote back telling her about Legless and the carry on at the parade. People wondered if Legless would ever get out of Ballinacora. It seems there was talk of giving him a new treatment of electric shocks with the hope of calming him. Any time he was let out of the mental hospital, he always went for the bishop. There seemed to be no end to his rage against the clergy. With time, people stopped talking about Legless but the corner boys still slagged Mr Delaney about his streaky bacon hair style, so he was delighted to get away on the morning of the second when Dad drove him, Mammy and Mrs Delaney to the airport.

The next day Garda Fallon was murdered. They were gone

to France and Daddy said, "Arlene, I'm sorry but I have to be in Dublin for the next few days on account of the murder."

"But Daddy, Mammy is in France."

"I know. Mrs McLoughlin is going to take care of you. Just be grateful your mother is in France."

"Why?"

"She's of a delicate nature. Things prey on her mind so it better she is out of the country and not listening to the news about the murder of the garda."

Dad had understood my sadness when Kait went away but now he didn't seem to realise I felt so lonely that even in my sleep I cried. Lots of mornings I woke up with tears on my pillow.

Evelyn and Ricky

Why couldn't things be the way they were before. Why did people have to go away and leave me? Even Ev, who was supposed to be with me in fifth year, was always with Ricky. She only came to school some days. As she had started drinking and smoking heavily like Ricky, even on those days she came to school, she was out of it and always complaining her head was killing her.

We spoke during the break when the other girls went downstairs to the yard, shutting ourselves into one of the presses in the cloakroom, so no one could hear her tell me all the things she and Ricky were up to after they left the pub and parked in an out-of-the-way spot.

"Why do ye do that?"

"So we can talk."

"Don't you do enough talking in the pub?"

"Yeah, we do but then me and Ricky do a bit of what the priests would call 'sins of impurity,' you know, I let him…"

I must have looked blank because she said exasperated, "… take his buddy out and rub it up and down in my hand when we are lying against each other."

It sounded disgusting and I was going to tell her she couldn't do that but then I remembered I wanted to melt into Michael's body, so I said, "Well, don't let it near your gigeen."

"I only touch it with my hand."

"How does it feel?"

"How do you think? Hot and clammy. Anyway after a minute of milking it in my hand, white stuff splatters out."

"On your hand!"

"Of course. Here they come. Let's get back," she said as we heard the girls coming up the stairs and I thought what a disgusting pig Ricky was and wondered if he drank a lot of milk to make his wee-wee white.

A week later in the next snatch of conversation, she told me they were exploring with her top and bra off.

"Ev, you can't do that."

"I can and I do."

"Be careful."

"Shut up. You sound like the priest in confession."

"Did you go to Fr Mannion?"

"I did like fun. I went to a priest in Galway."

The girls coming up the stairs cut the conversation short. I didn't hear any more about Ev and Ricky's love affairs until the middle of May.

Some evenings I went up to Úna's house in Dun na Rí Road instead of going to Late Study. As her house was always crawling with their relatives from the North, we used to go across the road to the cemetery and sit on one the tombstones to chat.

"How come you have so many cousins?" I asked her one evening.

"Because I do."

"I wish I had my house full of relatives like you do."

"And I wished I lived in a house like yours."

"Why. You'd have Mouth looking at you all the time."

"It wouldn't be so bad."

"Look, you're lucky because your father is always at home."

"Yeah, and he talks to you more than he does to me."

She sounded upset, so I changed the subject quickly. "I love that top you're wearing, Úna. That shade of blue really suits your colouring."

"Mrs Quinn's. Isn't it great she's a red head too? She has lovely expensive clothes, and she gives me so many it's unbelievable."

"You looked absolutely stunning."

"Maybe that why I have a guy after me."

"A fellow after you?"

"Yeah, he asked me to the cinema this Friday night."

"Who is he?"

"You wouldn't like him, but I don't care cos it's the first time a fellow has shown interest in me."

"Who? Paddy O'Neill?"

"No. You'll never guess so I'll tell you straight out."

"Quick, tell me."

"I'm doing the books in Quinn's, and we pay for lots of stuff by cheque which we send by post and it's me who takes the letters to the post office. He works there."

"You don't mean the gorgeous looking hunk from Cork who was going out with Noeleen this summer?" I asked, real surprised the Cork guy had asked Úna out.

New Guys in Town

In Drumbron when a new fellow started working in the bank, the Gardaí or the post office, girls would go to 'spot the talent,' hoping he notices them and asked them out. The fellows usually picked the good-looking girls from 'respectable' family to do a line with, while they tried to have their way with the other girls.

It happened everywhere because Mammy had been the girl chosen by Daddy in her home place. She was beautiful and came from a good family, so people weren't surprised she was the lucky girl among all the ones who lived in her area.

The Cork guy would have to be really in love with Úna to ask her out. Her ugly duckling years were gone, and she was getting more like a swan, but her family were not 'respectable.' Mammy would have kittens if she ever found out I was pals with a girl whose father was on the dole and whose brothers went to England to work on the building sites. These thoughts were in my mind which made me feel guilty but then Úna confirmed it when she said, "No, you silly goose, it's the other new fellow."

I was flabbergasted and looked at her with horror in my eyes. The other new fellow was so ugly that girls ran away from him and nick-named him 'Igor' after one of Frankenstein's servants in the Hammer horror films.

Igor had two rows of big, wide teeth in a loose mouth of thick lips. Then to make his mouth even uglier, two extra fang-like teeth grew in the gums on top of the front teeth and two more stuck out on the bottom row. When he smiles the whole set of teeth were on display making his mouth looked like a dog's. In addition, he had a long, pointy nose and bulgy fisheyes. I lowered my eyes quickly so she wouldn't see the shock in them.

"So, I mean… when did he ask you out?"

"Well, since I go to the post office every week, we are always talking and then it turns out Aloysius –"

I was so glad Ev wasn't around because the name Aloysius would have set her off.

"…is a member of the Vincent de Paul," finished Úna.

"Oh!"

"He and that Howlin man were in the widow McGrath's house on Wednesday."

"The McGrath's house is near yours?"

"Yeah. It's only two doors down from ours, so when he saw me in our garden…"

I thought, 'Yeah, to get away from all your Northern relations…'

"…he smiled, and we started talking."

"And?"

"He asked me if I wanted to go and see *Butch Cassidy and the Sundance Kid*."

"Úna, you were wearing your glasses, weren't you? Because you know he's not very good-looking."

"All cats are black at night," she said repeating what Ricky used to say about ugly girls.

"I wouldn't want to go out with him."

"It's alright for you, Arlene, you can be picky, but I'll be lucky if anyone else ever asks me out. That auld Howlin man would shag me down Castle Fields, but you can be sure he wouldn't let his son date me."

"I just mean…"

"I know what you meant. I should be like Elizabeth Bennet and wait for my Mr Darcy, but life has made me more of a Charlotte Lucas and a Mr Collins is fine for me."

"But we are…?"

"Women. I see my mother struggling every day. Since the factory closed and Dad lost his job, my wages is the only money Mam can count on to pay the rent."

"I know it's hard."

"You don't because you never saw your mother go without potatoes at dinner time."

"I'm sorry, Úna, I didn't know."

"Of course not but Mam goes without so as to give her food to the young ones."

"I…"

"Ar, I want a husband with a secure job for life or no husband at all. I don't want to worry about paying the light bill. I don't want to be nice to some dirty old pig from St Vincent's to get the 2/6."

"It's just…"

"Don't worry, I'm not marrying him."

"Oh good."

"Only because he didn't ask me. First a date and we'll take it from there."

If Úna started doing a line with Aloysius, then it would be me on my own because Sam and Nuala's souls had become bound together by the resin of the old manuscripts they loved. Ancient and dusty archives in draughty old monasteries and mansions made their eyes light up and their bodies move closer as they examined a reference they found to such-and-such a thing that proved their theory about such-and-such a manuscript being written by such-and-such an author.

Such academic things excited them as much as Ricky when a horse he backed won at incredible odds. The Irish language, in which they conversed, was the baby they loved with all the passion of the world, telling anyone who would listen that language shapes a person's thoughts and perception of reality. Such was their love for the Irish language that they sought and fought for a radio station that would broadcast in Irish to recuperate the soul that was lost because as they said, '*Tír gan teanga, tír gan anam.*' Which means, 'A country without a language is a country without a soul.'

When a pirate radio station called *Saor Raidió* began broadcasting, I suspected Nuala and Sam were involved in the running of it. They disappeared for long stretches of time but when I asked Nuala about it, she said the less I knew, the better.

Úna was spending time with Aloysius, so I was on my own most of the time, dreaming of Michael. I wondered if I should go to England to look for him.

To help me decide, I wrote to Angela McNamara, a woman who had a column at the back of the Sunday newspaper, asking her for advice. Before I posted the three-page letter, I showed it to Mrs Lynch.

"Arlene, you can't seriously consider taking the advice of that woman?"

"Why not?"

"Because a woman wrote to her saying her husband struck her across the face in front of the children."

"And?"

"She told the poor woman to stop being so selfish. She needed to love her husband more and show him she needed him."

"That's awful, Mrs Lynch."

"I know it is. No wonder women put up with so much having someone on the newspaper say that."

"I won't write to her then because the right thing was to tell the woman to leave her husband."

"I'm glad."

"Will you be my Angela and tell me what to do, Mrs Lynch?"

"I will my best for what's it worth."

"Well, I kissed Michael and I can't stop thinking about him."

"Kiss him again."

"I can't, he's gone to England."

"Write to him."

"I can't, I don't know where he is."

"What do you know about him."

"He's nice."

"Is he into sport?"

"I don't know, I just know I love him."

"Do you know if he likes reading?"

"I don't."

"You don't know much about him."

"I do. He kisses great."

"Do you know that song *All kinds of Everything reminds me of You* that won the Eurovision?"

"Of course I do. Since Dana won it's always on the radio."

"Well, you sing it and see how many things reminds you of your Michael."

I started singing it and realise very few of the things reminded me of him.

"What you feel for Michael is infatuation because you can only really love a person you know."

"How do you know that Mrs Lynch?"

"After the birth of my daughter, Mary Ann, I could do nothing."

"You poor thing."

"I had Declan. He was very good and minded the baby because I couldn't get out of bed. He was the one who changed her nappies."

"Wasn't he good, Mrs Lynch?"

"He was but if we hadn't more than kisses, he would have left."

"He didn't leave you, though."

"No, he stuck by a woman who couldn't even give birth to a child without getting sick for life."

"Mrs Lynch, it wasn't your fault you had a difficult birth."

"My mother had ten babies and she didn't end up like me, not able to walk right or to go outside the door."

"Ten children, that's a lot."

"I only had one and without Declan, I don't know what I'd have done."

"He made you the easel."

"He's the best man there is. We still talk and listen to the matches together."

"So ye like the game? I only watch football when Dad is at home. When he's not around I don't care if I never saw a match."

"Me and Declan are the opposite, we love it. Galway, with Lamb as the captain, is sure to win the Sam McGuire."

"What else do ye talk about?" I asked her as talking about football bored me.

"Books, Declan is a great reader, and he loves the cinema."

"But you can't go."

"No, but when there a picture on television we watch it together and talk about it. Declan thinks John Ford is the best film director that ever existed."

"When I go to the pictures, I only go to see the actors. I never even thought directors were important."

"You do but you don't know you do. Hitchcock?"

"I love his films."

"So you see, directors are important."

Mrs Lynch reminded me of Nan and Nanny. She was down-to-earth and clever like they were. If they were alive and on

Clonthu Hill, I'd go and tell them the farthings and halfpennies that they kept in their pouches hanging between their biddies were gone out of circulation.

The coins were gone like my friends. Even Mammy was gone to Lourdes and Dad to Dublin. I was on my own. I was thinking this and feeling sorry for myself as I headed to Mrs McLoughlin's house for my dinner. Daddy had arranged for me to have my meals in Mrs McLoughlin's house on Kilmartin Road while he and Mammy were away. He had also suggested that Mrs McLoughlin, the housekeeper, slept in our house so I would not be alone, but I had stamped my foot and insisted I was big and didn't need a babysitter.

Mrs McLoughlin was standing at her front door waiting for me. It was then that I realised everything hadn't changed. Mrs McLoughlin, with her wrap-around apron, was still the same, minding me like she used to do when I was small.

That same evening after Late Study, I went to her house and had a bowl of hot semolina with sugar and cold milk the same as the McLoughlins were having. When they were finished, Catherine and Paddy went upstairs to sleep. It was time for me to go home to my bed. The thought of spending the night in my empty house was frightening. When Mrs McLoughlin saw me dragging my feet and walking slowly she said, "Mary, if you don't mind sleeping with Catherine, you could stay here." I didn't answer, just ran and hugged her. We went to my house and got my things. Mrs McLoughlin must have felt the buzzing that was inside me because she warned me not to make noise going up the stairs. I didn't, even though my feet wanted to dance, celebrating that I had a sister to sleep with in the bed like my friends.

Catherine was already asleep when I crept in beside her. There was a sheet on the bottom of the bed but none on top, only a thin, pink blanket with two white stripes at the edge. The blanket, touching my chin, was rough but I didn't care because the bed wasn't cold and empty. A soft warmness like a hot water bottle came from Catherine. I stayed on my side of the bed, not wanting to take up too much room. Catherine must have sensed me because she moved towards me. The heat of her body was cosy and comforting. I fell asleep happy. During the night, the cold woke me up. Catherine had rolled over and pulled the blankets off me. I moved close to her back. I fell asleep and dreamt. In my dream, the figure I was snuggling up against was Liam. When I woke up in the morning, I was holding Catherine around the waist and there was a smile on my face.

I went downstairs with my hair falling about my face. Mrs McLoughlin didn't tell me to pull it back or follow me around with a brush and a hairband. I sat at the table where Paddy and Catherine were fighting for the same slice of toast. They were the only two McLoughlin children left at home.

The ten days I stayed in the family took away all my loneliness. I was part of a family with Mrs McLoughlin smiling when I came in the door asking her what was for dinner.

The first day we had crubeens boiled with the cabbage and boiled potatoes. The cabbage had a lovely taste, and it was great picking up the small knuckly things in my hands and nibbling at salty, pink, jelly-like meat on the bones.

Mrs McLoughlin was faster than Speedy Gonzalez the way she stuck a fork into a hot spud, held it with her thumb and ran a knife around the skin until it was white and floury. She loosened it from the fork, and it dropped onto the plate.

When I came in from Late Study she asked if I managed to get all my lessons done before serving me stir-about which could be porridge, tapioca or the semolina I had the first night. Then it was time for bed.

One evening Mrs McLoughlin told me about Michael and Jim in London. She said Jim, the youngest, was the cutest of her two boys. After arriving in London, like most boys from Ireland, he worked on the buildings as a labourer. Shortly afterwards, he found out about a scheme, where people who had worked in obsolete trades, could retrain. Saying he was a thatcher when he lived in Ireland, he was eligible to retrain, and he had Michael apply too. Now the McLoughlin boys were qualified carpenters.

Another evening she showed me photos of Maura in her nursing uniform. She was proud her daughter was a qualified nurse.

"You know Maura could be working as a nurse if she wanted to but instead, she is doing midwifery."

"Why does she want to be a midwife?"

"Well, it will be easier for her to find work here in Ireland."

"Is it hard to get a job as a nurse?" I asked surprised.

"If you have pull, it's not."

"Ricky Martin said he's getting a job as a manager in the Regional Hospital when he does his Leaving."

"He'll have no trouble finding a good job with his father a TD. And yourself, Mary, are you still wanting to be an artist?"

"How did you know, Mrs McLoughlin?" I asked delighted that someone knew what I wanted to do.

"Sure weren't you always the great little painter. I still have that picture of the little boy your mother was going to throw out."

"Ah, go away!"

She went to a box on the dresser and took out the picture of Will that I painted when I was sick with the measles.

"Oh my God, you kept it." I was wiping the tears away with the back of my hand because they had started to fall for no reason.

"Mary, that soft heart of yours will be your undoing," she said as she put it back in the box but the look in her eye told me she was glad I was soft-hearted.

After the first night Catherine and I went upstairs every night together, chatting for ages before we went to sleep. One night I told her I was going to see Mrs Lynch the following day.

She surprised me by saying, "Don't go near her house!"

"Why?"

"The woman who lives there is odd. She's a witch."

"She's not a witch. Why do you say that about her?"

"She never goes out."

"She can't go out because she's sick."

"She isn't. Mrs Kennedy hears her shuffling around the house."

"She has difficulty walking."

"Yeah, I know. It's because her legs got frozen when the Titanic sank."

"She wasn't on the Titanic."

"She was. It was built in Belfast and the ones up there wrote the numbers and letters on the side of the ship so the reflection in the water said, 'No Pope.'"

"It sank because it hit an iceberg."

"Well, it sank anyway so that Mrs Lynch woman couldn't get on the lifeboat. She swam back to Kerry."

"If you say so. Anyway, I'm calling in to see her. Do you want to come?"

"I don't know… but I'll show you where she lives, if you want."

"I know where she lives."

"I mightn't go into the house with you, if you don't mind."

As usual, Mrs Lynch was delighted to see me. I showed her the letter I got from Kait and told her I was with the McLoughlin's while Mammy was in Lourdes.

"How's your friend Úna?"

"I don't see much of her since she started working. Before I'd go to her house but now it's always full of her relations from Derry and Belfast, so it's not the same."

"And couldn't you become friends with her cousins?"

"They are all men, no girl cousins. It's hard to understand them and besides, they are always talking of stupid things like the Arms Trial."

"True, they have their own way of talking. Look, there's Fluffy, back from his visit to his cousins in Delia's. Will your mother be back soon?"

"The day after tomorrow, Mrs Lynch."

People in Wheelchairs

Mammy loved everything in France except the people in the wheelchairs. She said the place where Our Lady appeared was packed with sick people and invalids wearing dowdy clothes that didn't impress her at all. Even the blankets they had wrapped around them were uninspiring.

When they arrived at the guest house-type accommodation, Mammy was tired and fell asleep as soon as she went to bed. The next morning when she went to the dining room, she saw Mrs Delaney sitting at a table with some nuns. They were passing around little, plastic statue bottles of Our Lady full of holy water. The nuns were from Donegal, and they had discovered the cutest little chapel where they heard Mass every morning. Mrs Delaney wanted to stay with them instead of going to Paris and got into a huff after breakfast, saying she wasn't budging from the guesthouse.

Mr Delaney only persuaded his mother to get into the taxi by telling her they would make a detour to the stall of the plastic Virgins, so she and two of her new friends could buy some bottles. The taxi waited while Mrs Delaney and her friends stocked up on holy water and rosary beads. Then they drove the nuns back. Mammy and Mouth had a hard time preventing Mrs Delaney from following them. The taxi driver was only too happy to deposit his warring passengers at the station where the train was about to depart.

"Ye were so lucky ye didn't miss the train," said Ev who was in our house to see if there were any souvenirs for her. She was disappointed because even though Mrs Delaney had filled her case with holy water bottles, they were for her own friends. We continued listening as they told us how the three of them jumped onto the train while the nuns called after them that they would pray the hotel in Paris was as nice as their guest house. The nun's prayers were answered because according to Mammy, the Parisian hotel was divine.

"The Royal Hotel here in Drumbron is nothing compared to the heavenly hotel that we stayed in. It had a lift even though we didn't use it. We were on the first floor looking out onto a street they call a 'rue' full of shops called boutiques. I'm sure Jackie shops in the Parisian boutiques."

"So ye enjoyed yourselves among the French?" Mrs McLoughlin asked.

"The French might know about what 'chic' is and they are fashionable, but they could do with learning English," Mammy said.

Mrs Delaney added, "And learning how to make a decent cup of tea. That first morning in Paris when we sat down to breakfast, they placed a long box of different type of teas they called 'tisanes' but not a bag of Lydon's tea could I see among the lot. The Donegal nuns had their own tea bags with them but ye wouldn't let me stay with them," she said giving Mr Delaney and Mammy awful looks.

"Mother!"

"John, you might have liked those sweet things they called 'croissant' first thing in the morning, but I wanted a nice slice of toast like I had with the nuns," Mrs Delaney complained

"Mother, on the continent they have continental breakfast, that's why they give coffee and a roll."

"They can have what they like once they learn how to make tea. I was parched for the want of a decent sup of tea," Mrs Delaney said.

"Mother, you should have had the coffee like I told you. It was wonderful. It reminded me of Rome and the little sidewalk cafes."

"Spending time in Paris is making Mouth sound affected," Ev whispered to me, "but that idea he has of opening a travel agency in Drumbron is a great idea. Mam could get a job there."

After that day I didn't see Ev again until the beginning of May. I was surprised to see her on Sligo Road waiting for me, like she and Kait used to do before. I bounced across the street and hugged her.

"Hey, don't break me."

"Oh Ev, I'm so happy to see you. I missed you so much."

"Yeah, I don't want to have to stay back and do fifth year again, so here you have me."

"I'm so glad, we have the exams at the beginning of June so you'll..."

"Pass my exams with flying colours because I'm going to charm the life out of the teachers and in case that fails, I'll have a few little slips of paper with the answers written on them."

"You don't need to cheat."

"Just in case. I hadn't a notion of repeating, it's bad enough with Ricky being kept back every year without me staying back as well."

"Sure, he never goes to school, so how can he pass?"

"Stop talking about him. I'm sick to the teeth of that fellow."

"I don't believe you."

"Believe me because I hate him. He is pestering me to go the whole way."

"The whole way where?"

"The whole way inside me. I kept forgetting you don't have a clue about boys. Anyway last night he asked me to take my knickers off so his bud could touch my... you know..."

"I hope you didn't!"

"I sorta did. Then he started saying I had to let him put it in."

I was going to ask, "Where?" but then knew she meant her gigeen because I remember there was a soft feeling in my gigeen when I was leaning against Michael, so I just said, "Don't for the life of you."

"I couldn't cos when he pressed it hurt, so we stopped."

I was worried and was going to tell her not to let him put his buddy into her gigeen, but we heard Mary O'Rourke and Cora Rushe coming behind us, so I just whispered, "Be careful."

From then Ev was waiting for me every morning and told me how far they had gone the previous evening in their exploring of each other's bodies. At first, they kept their clothes on but little by little more was bared, and Ricky was poking her gigeen with his buddy.

"Ev, make him stop or he'll get in."

"Don't worry he can't because when he pokes it hurts, so we stop."

Around the time we were doing our exams, which was about a month after the poking has started, she said it didn't hurt anymore.

"He's saying I have to let him put it in."

"Don't. You have already gone too far with him."

"If I don't, one of the girls who fancies him will."

"It doesn't matter. You are his girlfriend, and you are going to get engaged when he finishes school remember."

"I suppose. At least now I have the excuse of the exams for not drinking and for going home early."

Ev was wild but she also was very brainy, so she learned quicker than some girls who had had their noses stuck in the books all year.

Nuala was smart too, but she wasn't wild and spent her evenings reading. As Sam was reading history at Trinity College, the two of them loved talking about political stuff. Nuala's way of speaking was beginning to sound stilted, like the books she read. Even Fr Mannion gave her a funny look when she told him, "Father, Arlene and I have decided to pass the baton on to the younger generation."

"And what baton might that be, Miss McCabe?" he said, knowing well she was speaking about the youth club.

"Father, we are renouncing our position on the board of the youth club committee."

"So I won't be seeing ye around, is that what you are saying, Miss McCabe."

"Yes Father, Arlene and I are resigning."

We finished our exams at the end of June. Ev was happy because now she could be off all the time with Ricky.

While she was falling deeper in love with Ricky, I was forgetting about Michael. I had spent all fifth year thinking about Michael. He was all I thought about when I was alone, and the letters I would write to him if I had his address. When I wrote the letters in my head, I realised I didn't know what to write to him.

Kait read the same type of books as me and went to the same pictures, but I didn't know if Michael was into books or if he liked the cinema. I didn't even know what songs he listened to or if he had nice manners when he ate. All I knew were that his lips felt soft, and my body wanted to melt into his body. I thought about our kiss every second of every minute until my mind couldn't take any more.

He was like a sweet cake I had stuffed myself with and couldn't eat another piece without getting sick and vomiting. When I told Mrs Lynch she said, "There's a lot of sense in the old saying, 'Too much of a good thing is bad for you'."

"Kait is something good and I'm dying for her to come."

Both of us had a letter from Kait saying she was getting a week's holidays the last week in August.

"I couldn't have got better news. No, I tell a lie. If I had a letter from Mary Ann saying she was coming, that would be the best news I could ever get."

Mrs Lynch's daughter, Mary Ann, had gone to America to work in a family as a nanny. She met a Polish man at the local Catholic church. They got married and now had three children. It was too expensive for them to come home on holidays.

Mrs Lynch used to say it was the fate of Irish mothers to rear their children for export.

"Arlene, I hope you never have to emigrate."

"My mother wouldn't let me. Mrs Lynch, who's knows, maybe one day Mary Ann will come home on holidays like Kait."

"Maybe someday but as least we'll see Kait."

"Well you mightn't see much of us because when Dad is home from Dublin, I'll have his car and we'll be off to every dance there is."

"Ya little devil. I might surprise you and meself and Delia will go along with ye too!"

Talking to Mrs Lynch was great craic but Nuala was another story, a boring one. Sometimes I couldn't take her spiels about the Civil Rights Movement.

"Arlene, as Sam says, this is the first time since Partition that the people in the North are finding their voice and expressing their outrage against the injustice and discrimination in housing, jobs and their right to vote."

I nodded my head but kept moving away. I needed to laugh and act the eejit to stop me worrying about what Evelyn was doing with Ricky. She was off with Ricky most days and nights and making me an expert on what goes on in the back seat of a car on a boreen on a warm, summer night.

"Now that weather is warm, it's great because my skin isn't covered in goosepimples."

"Ev, you say the strangest of things! Why would your skin be covered in goosepimples?"

"Sometimes I think you're really stupid. When Ricky starts peeling my clothes off, I'm shivering, covered in goosepimples until we get into it."

"You don't undress completely, do you?"

"I do, stark naked."

"Oh, Ev! At least leave your underwear on."

"I don't take them off."

"Good," I sighed.

"It's Ricky who takes them off."

"Evelyn!"

"Shut up. Anyhow he knows what he's doing." How could she believe that stupid *amadán* who didn't know anything about anything? "What does he know?"

"It. You know…"

Ricky hadn't a clue above anything except drinking.

"He always pulls out before he comes."

"Pulls out what?"

"You are such a baby, Arlene. It means he comes out from inside me before he jerks off, so nothing will happen, and I won't get into trouble."

I didn't really know what she meant by 'jerking off' so all I said was, "Be careful." She was doing what you can only do when you are married. If Mammy or Mouth found out, they would tell Batt the postman, who in turn would let Fr Mannion know. Everyone knew the priest believed unchaste women were better locked up in a laundry than walking around, tempting men to sin.

I went to Úna's house to talk to her about my worries. Mr McNulty was there and foaming at the mouth, so I didn't get a chance to talk, only to listen to him giving out stink about what had happened in the Falls.

"The feicers had no right to go smashing down doors! They didn't leave a teapot they didn't break or a mattresses they didn't rip to bits. Looking for weapons my arse!"

Mr McNulty was talking about the police who had gone on a rampage, breaking windows, windscreens and battering down doors with batons and pickaxes, while men in long, blackcoats beat people on the streets who hadn't galloped fast enough to get inside a house and close the door.

Sam sam-ified it and said, "The British Army entered the Falls as ruthless aggressors, harassing the local population under the pretence that they were searching for weapons. When the residents protested against the house-to-house search, CS gas was fired at them."

What Sam said was true. On the news we saw the soldiers firing CS gas at the people. The poor things stumbled around, the gas burning their eyes and making breathing difficult. The CS gas turned the Falls into a smouldering hell that no one could leave. A mob, wielding clubs, some stubbed with nails, helped the police ensure no locals left the area. The Falls area became a jail, with the locals locked into their neighbourhood. The siege lasted from the 3rd to the 5th of July.

I found all this reminiscent of what Nan and Nanny had told us about the Black and Tans. However, I was frightened to voice my opinions as Mammy wasn't interested in the terrible things that were happening in the North. Any outrage she and her golf friends felt was not directed at the British Army but at John Lennon who had invited a group of hippies to establish a commune on his Island of Dorinish.

"Why do we have to have these hippies? Aren't they causing enough trouble in America with their drugs without us having to tolerate them in Ireland?"

"Mammy, I heard Nuala and Sam saying it a good way of repopulating the islands."

"And build councils houses for them with the money your father pays in tax, I suppose?"

Sam wouldn't have agreed with Mammy. He was saying people living on Dorinish would keep the traditional style of life alive. Nuala said she might go there to teach the folk in the community the Irish language.

I was sure they'd gone to the island but then I caught a glimpse of what I thought was Nuala's face on TV in the Andersonstown March. Thousands of women and kids marched from Andersonstown with food and groceries for the locals of the

Falls. I'd swear I saw Nuala among the women and imagined Sam was beside her, with a scarf tied around his head, disguised as a woman.

"I loved to be with them," I told Úna when I met her at the Odeon cinema.

"I wouldn't. Imagine having to listen to Nuala telling the Belfast women they should organise a Samuel Beckett Quiz."

Úna and I met every Monday night to go to the pictures. The Monday we went to see *The Pit and Pendulum* I asked her about her boyfriend.

"And Aloysius? How are things between the two of ye?"

"Great, honestly. He's a lovely fellow."

"So he'll be introduced to your family soon?"

"No way. Do you want my father to frighten him off with his going on about Haughey and Blaney having to resign? Until he pops the question, he's not going near my father."

"And keep him away from Sam too."

"You can be sure I will. I'll get the tickets, wait near the door."

As she moved away a guy bumped against me.

"Sorry."

"No harm done," I answered.

"You know it's your fault I bumped against you."

"What do you mean?" I asked but knowing he was slagging because of the glint in his eye.

"I couldn't see right because your beauty blinded me."

"Shut up!" but I was laughing because I liked him. His accent wasn't from around, so I said, "Where are you from?"

"Longford."

"And what are you doing here?"

"Staying with my cousins, the McNally's." Then I realised he was a fine-looking hunk like the four or five McNally brothers who were John Wayne bodied men with Ryan O'Neil type faces.

"How long are you staying?" I surprised myself by asking so many questions and he surprised me by answering them.

"I'll be here for the Galway races. Tomorrow I'm driving to Sligo but I'm not too sure what road to take."

"I was thinking of going myself so if…" I said that even though I hadn't thought about going until that minute.

"If you let me give you a lift, you could show me the way."

"Great, save me getting the bus."

I introduced him to Úna and the three of us watched the film *The Pit and Pendulum* together. The film made me jump and lean against Paddy.

Thanks to the stranger from Longford, July was the best month I had since the Inter Cert. That Exam had changed the direction of my life and my friends' lives, as if it were a crossroads. It sent each of us down a different road and I was left standing on my own without my childhood friend Kait and only seeing Úna every now and then.

Thanks to Paddy, the heaviness was fading, and the days were taking on a sweet, mellow hue. I purred in the warmth and light from the summer sun and in the attentiveness from this gorgeous guy. In Sligo, we kissed on Strand Hill beach as the waves roared and crashed against the rocks. The second kiss of my life. This kiss was different from my first kiss. It lacked the surprise and the incredulity of the tingling that just the touch of Michael's lips on mine had sent through my entire body.

My second kiss was lovely, but it didn't make me go weak at the knees.

When I went to see Mrs Lynch, I told her I didn't understand how I could fancy Paddy when only a few months earlier I had been sad for Michael.

"Arlene, do you eat the same kind of food all the time?"

"Of course not, I eat plenty of different things."

"And do you like everything the same?"

"No, I love chips and mashed potatoes with loads of butter more than I like cabbage."

"So Michael was your mashed potatoes and Paddy is your chips. Just as you can enjoy different types of food, you can love different boys."

"But you married Declan because you loved him."

"I do but before him I was in love plenty of times. People think love is like a dress that you have to wear for ever. Arlene, you are only sixteen…"

"Nearly seventeen."

"So there's plenty of time for you to find the love of your life when you are older."

"You might be right, Mrs Lynch. Sure as they say, 'There's plenty of fish in the sea.'"

"There is, so off with ya and enjoy the time you have with that young lad before he goes home to Longford."

When Paddy left at the end of July, I wasn't heartbroken like the time Mouth Delaney had forced Michael to leave.

The truth is, I couldn't be anything only cheerful as I was dying to see Kait. I wanted her to see my car and for her to come places with me while she was home in August. While I waited for her to arrive, I did my best not to listen to Mr McNulty giving out about the British Army using plastic bullets on civilians in the North.

My Own Car

Dad had bought me a second-hand car. I had felt really touched when he apologised for the car not being a brand new one, like Loretta's red Mini.

"Arlene, it's just an old banger."

"I don't care, Dad. It's so wonderful having a car."

"You'll have to prove yourself next week."

"Do you actually want me to drive to Cavan? You won't be afraid to sit in beside me?"

Dad was fine on the trip to Aunt Hazel's house, but Mammy was the typical backseat driver. I spent my time reassuring her I knew what I was doing but to no avail, so when we got to Carrick-On-Shannon, I asked Dad to sit behind the wheel and drive the reast of the way to get Mammy off my back.

We spent a week in Cavan. Mammy loved the Farnham Arms Hotel where we went for lunch. Dad pointed out that the convent where the children were burned in 1943 was close by. My mother got very annoyed saying he used any chance he could to criticise the Catholic church instead of stopping to think of the great work the Poor Clare's did. I saw by the expression of surprise on his face that it hadn't been his intention to offend, and her angry outburst baffled him. That might have been the reason he only asked me to go with him to an event in a Protestant hall.

Protestantism in Ireland

The evening was a lecture about Protestantism in Ireland. We sat in the back row, which turned out to be the best, because when the speaker said the English had come to Ireland to civilise the Irish, I tightened up like a coil ready to spring at the man. I felt Dad's hand on my shoulder. It kept me from jumping up, but I looked at him questioning this outrageous statement and my eyes said, "That's not true."

I sat in stony silence listening to the lies about how the Protestant religion had a transforming effect on the barbarian Irish and how a new social order was created. I clamped my mouth shut as the lecturer said we, the Irish, were so stupid that we tied the rope onto the horse's tail when we ploughed the land.

Naturally, at the end of the lecture I didn't clap. I waited for the 'Any Questions' like is asked at the end of a conference in Drumbron. I was ready to tell the lecturer half of what he had said were lies, but I didn't get the chance. It was not the custom to ask questions.

When the entertainment started my annoyance dispersed, floating away as I listened to the girl playing the accordion. As a singer started singing *My Old Orange Flute*, I opened my mouth to sing along but I felt the touch of my father's hand on my arm. It was pity because I knew the song, the Clancy's and the Dubliners had a version of it, and we used to play it in the youth club. When the concert was over, I stood up and clapped.

The lights in the hall came on. I thought that was it and we'd go home. However, some ladies came from the room behind the stage carrying trays of tea, buns and slices of cake. This was different too. In Drumbron, a table would be set up and people would help themselves to whatever they liked as often as they liked.

In Drumbron, there was an old lady known as the Cake Grabber who slipped buns and cake into her bag when she thought no one was looking. She wouldn't have been able to do it here as everyone remained seated holding the cups daintily in their hands and the slice of cake on the saucer. Dad got up telling me to stay sitting and drink my tea. He went and spoke to different men he knew. I didn't get a chance to talk to him until we were on the way back to Aunt Hazel's house.

"The people in that hall are so stupid, Dad. Don't they know we had our culture, language and the Brehon Laws."

"Arlene, everyone is entitled to their point of view."

"They are but without telling lies."

"Arlene, please!" He used an impatient tone he had never used before with me. "That hall holds very dear memories. My father and my grandfather attended it. I was a member too, but when I married your mother, I had to leave it."

"So did you bring me there to see how they think and for me to know you are different?"

"Different! My education taught me to be how I am."

"Like them? So you want me to understand their way of seeing things?" I asked nodding my head in the direction of the hall we had just left.

"No, I want you to see there are two types of Irish people, each with their own history."

"Their own... your history is not true."

"It is. My ancestors came to Ireland thinking they were bringing the true religion to the inhabitants of this island."

"Like our priests go to the missions to convert the heathens."

"The missions, of course not."

"Dad, I'm not stupid. I heard them say we were savages."

"I know well you're not stupid. So telling you about the importance religion played in the political changes in Europe won't go over your head."

"The Thirty-Year War."

"That especially. The English planters believed they had a religious mission to defend civility and genuine Christianity. For them, the state's interest…"

"The English State, you mean?"

"Yes, the interest of the Crown and the true religion went together. That is why they wanted unity between the island of Ireland and England."

"Great, so to do that, you get rid of the natives and plant people who are loyal. The Normans didn't." At that moment, I realise my surname was Norman. "Hey Dad, the Blake's came with the Normans, not the English."

He laughed when I said that. "You are nobody's fool. What I want you to know is that you are special."

"Special?"

"Yes, the future in the present."

"What?"

"In a few generations most Irish will be like you, a mixture."

I looked at him and thought how clever he was because he was right. Nuala was a mixture too and she didn't think like my mother or Mr Delaney.

"With people like you, the churches will lose the power they have."

"Dad, I can't believe you're so clever," I said happy to know he had brought me to the Orange Hall not to make me be different than what I was but to show I was a bridge between the two cultures of Ireland.

Aunt Hazel had a party while I was in Cavan and invited lots of people my age. She introduced me to a few boys who were at Trinity with my cousin, Sam. I danced and laughed and had fun with the boys, but I felt nothing special towards any of them.

The day we went for a picnic to Lough Oughter, one called Johnathan never left my side. He said he'd love to come to see me any time Sam was visiting my house. I told him as I was doing my Leaving, I'd be too busy and got rid of him that way.

News for Kait

Kait arrived in Drumbron two days after I got back from Cavan. Úna, pushing one of the Quinn kids in a pushchair and dragging another by the hand, joined Ev minus Ricky, Nuala minus Sam and I who were waiting on the platform for Kait's train to pull in.

A dollybird, wearing a white fur coat with a pink mini dress that looked plastic, stood at the open train door, holding a beige suitcase, by a brassy looking handle. Her long golden hair shone around her pale glowing skin. Enormous eyes, made greener by the pink-lilac shadow, sparkled under heavy black lashes. Kait's pale-pink washed lips sang a shriek of delight as she jumped from the train and hugged us all in turn.

"You look gorgeous. I love your dress! God, it's buttoned all the way down the front and has a collar like a shirt," said Úna, who looked good herself in a tawny shift dress she had gotten from Mrs Quinn.

"Because it's a shirt dress, my dear Úna."

"It didn't take you long to become trendy, did it, Miss Kenny?" I slagged.

"Money maketh the man. Clothes are lots cheaper in England. Believe it or not, I have another shirt dress like this in blue."

"Where did you get the coat? Is it really fur?" Ev wanted to know.

"It's rabbit. All the girls wear them in Liverpool, so I saved and bought one to surprise ye."

"You sure have. The dress looks plastic."

"No, it's shiny material. Hey look, do ye like my block-heel shoes?"

We all looked at the white shoes with rounded toes. A stump of a heel came a third of the way down the sole of the shoe. It wasn't narrow and pointy like our stilettos. After we oohed and aahed about the shoes, Kait opened her mouth to show us the fillings she had in her back teeth.

"I got all my bad teeth filled because the dentist is free in England."

"You mean you don't have to pay?"

"No, nothing."

"Are you sure? My filling at the back cost me 7/6," Ev said.

Úna said, "My brother was dying with an awful toothache, and it cost my poor mother 2/6 to get the dentist to pull it out."

"Well, it's free in England and the doctor is too."

"That's great. Pity it's not like that here."

"Everyone has money in England."

I picked up her case and we left the station. As we walked to Kait's house in Kilmartin Road, we told her of the plans for the week.

"You will be the Belle of the Ball when you step out in one of those outfits."

"I'm dying to go dancing to show ye how the English girls dance."

"Are you up for going to see The Miami Showband in Sligo?"

"Of course I am! Look I want to have as much fun as I can while I'm at home because I won't be going out when I get back to the hospital."

"Fantastic. We'll tell this year Leaving Cert girls to keep us five seats on their bus."

"Four, I'm not sure I can go," Nuala said. We understood. She had been so busy planning an American Wake for Kait that she hadn't had time to make placards or protest about anything the whole week.

"Well, if you change your mind, there'll always be room on the bus."

"Kait, Nuala has planned an American Wake for you this weekend. You know she into all the old Irish customs and is trying to get us to wear shawls like Nan and Nanny used to," Ev slagged.

"That's not true. I just thought you'd like a party while you're here," Nuala said.

"But the American Wakes were for the people who went away and never came back again. I'll be home every summer."

"It doesn't matter. Sam and I are members of The Lost Heritage Club. Its aim is to revive old customs."

"Are we having my wake at the youth club this Friday?" Kait asked.

"No, it has to be at the family home or in a house at least, so it's at your house on Friday night. Your mother is over the moon about it."

"I'm in charge of the party food," Evelyn said.

"Party food?"

"You know cream crackers and slices of ham and cheese cut into small square on cocktail sticks with grapes in between."

"It sounds great."

"We're having bit of a *Buile Ruile* singsong sorta thing and we are going to dress up."

"Dress up?"

"Yeah, because you missed the fancy-dress competition."

"Thanks, girls, ye are too good. It's going to be like when we were small and had the plays out the back."

"Sorta. We hope you don't mind but we asked Delia and Maggie to come over."

"Not at all. Sure if there any of the fancy food left over, we could bring it to Mrs Lynch."

"Of course. As you can see, we have been making plans for you and to top it off, we are going to see The Miami on Saturday."

"Dickie Rock! It's going to be great!"

"By the way, Maura McLoughlin is home, so we are inviting her to the American Wake too."

"Stop calling it a wake, it's a party!"

Before Kait went into her own house, I arranged to meet her later in Sligo Road, so we could go for a walk and have a chat about Jim Smith.

We ended up in Castle Fields, sitting on the bridge, our bottoms pushed back on the stone wall so as to be more comfortable. Kait's legs dangled but mine were nearly touching the grassy ground. The sound of the river was soothingly familiar, gushing past, giving me the courage to tell Kait about Jim.

"Kait, Jim…" She turned her face to gaze intensely at me when I mentioned Jim. It was so as not to miss a syllable about the boy she had loved since she was a small girl, which made me falter. "He's… he`s doing… he's doing a line with Loretta."

"He can't be."

"I'm afraid he is."

"I don't believe you." She put her hands over her ears.

"Kait, listen please. I can assure you he is with Loretta."

"It's not true."

"It is. Just listen to me for a minute."

"Are you positive it's true?" She asked but shook her head as though wanting me to say it wasn't.

"I am.

"But when…"

"They used to play tennis together last summer."

"But that was last year, so it was. And maybe now they are not together?"

"At the moment, Loretta is in France."

"You see, they are not doing a line."

"They are. She is only in France because she has been perfecting her French…"

"More in her line to perfect her stupidity. So, if she's in France, Jim's not with her."

"But only because she's away. He's just waiting for her to return."

"He isn't, so he isn't. Anyway, how do you know? Maybe he's delighted she is gone."

"I know cos Mammy never shuts up about the dinner party the Fitzgeralds are having this Friday in the golf club. Jim is on the same table as the Fitzgerald family as Loretta's boyfriend."

"Her boyfriend? I don't believe it."

"They are always together, driving around in her new red Mini."

"Has she a car?"

"Yeah, her father bought her a brand new Mini in Smith's garage. I mean, in Smith's Automobile Dealership."

"Imagine her having a car and my father doesn't even have a bike."

She looked so downhearted that I said, "I'll teach you to drive in my car."

"I don't want to learn to drive."

"Why not?"

"Cos I'll never have a car."

"You will."

"I won't, but even if I had one, a lot of good it would do me because you said Jim is with Loretta."

"It's only because his family live near Loretta's, and their fathers play golf together."

"And my father doesn't."

"Let's forget about them. Driving is great fun."

"Are you going to teach me in a week?"

"Of course."

"So I have a week to learn but what's the use if we don't have a car?"

"Like I said, you'll have money."

"When?"

"When you are a nurse."

"I hope real nursing is better than what I am doing now."

"Don't you like it? Is it not nice?"

"Making beds, feeding people and washing their bodies, and on top of all that, some of the nuns are awful, giving us pucks in the back."

"Forget about them for the week you are here."

In spite of all her talk about not wanting to learn to drive, Kait was a natural. By the end of the week, we were whizzing up and down Suileen Lane and even ventured out on to Sligo Road.

On Friday Kait said, "Arlene, you are great teacher. Look at how well I can park? The wheels don't go up on the path now."

"You're so good, you're going to drive a bit of the way when we go to Sligo this evening to get my costume for the party."

"The Wake, you mean? They'll know what a wake is when I appear with this lonely face and my outfit."

"What are you going as?"

"A Banshee. I'm backcombing my hair and letting it drop all over my face and rubbing flour into my face. Mammy gave me an old sheet. I cut a hole in it, so I have the perfect dress. What are you going as?"

"A Viking. I ordered a long blonde wig in that fancy dress place in Sligo."

Kait drove to Sligo but didn't know where the shop was, so we stopped on the outskirts of the town, and I took over. I parked outside the door, and we rushed in to get my wig. It was a golden blonde one with a split in the middle and two long plaits.

Before going back to Drumbron, we had tea and a snack in a café near the river. Kait said she had passed the place a lot the summers she worked in the guest house. Back then she used to dream that Jim would take her there one day for a coffee.

"I know I'm not as handsome as Jim, but will I do?"

"Of course you will, you silly goose, but Arlene, I hope he gets tired of Loretta."

"I betcha he will. A lump of Chester cake is bigger than her."

"And more intelligent."

"Look at the time! Come on, let's get going."

After the drive back from Sligo, I dropped Kait off at her house. Nuala and Ev were there making sandwiches and getting things ready for the party. I told them I'd be back in a sec with my fancy dress on.

I galloped into my house carrying the bag with the wig and was half up the stairs when I heard Dad saying, "Arlene, are you too big to give your Dad a kiss?"

"Hello Dad, I thought you'd be in the barracks!" I said and turned back down and went into the kitchen taking my wig out and putting it on my head. "Dad, do you see how Norman I look, and it's not the wig, it's the Blake blood."

"Ach if Sam saw you, he'd think you were his mother. Hazel used to have long, blonde hair when we were children."

"Dad, talking about Sam… He says plastic bullets shouldn't be used against people."

"Surely Sam knows that plastic bullets will only be used as a last resort."

"No, they are being fired all the time."

"If they are, it is to maintain law and order." Before I could answer him, Mammy appeared with Mouth Delaney. I took the wig off and said I had to get ready for a party with Evelyn and Nuala, forgetting to mention Úna or Kait.

The Blonde Blake

I made sure I made a grand entrance into Kenny's kitchen, walking tall in brown, knee-high boots under a beige mini dress, my blonde plaits falling on each side of my chest.

"God between us and all harm! Is that you yourself Brigid that is in it?" Delia gasped in a wheezy voice.

"Delia, it's me, Arlene."

"For a minute I thought you were Brigid."

"Who is Brigid?"

"One of the little girls from the Home. She was a shy, little creature that minded her brother and she, herself, only a few years older than him."

"Why did you think I was her?" I asked surprised because no one ever spoke about the Home Babies. The truth was I was happy she did because sometimes I still dreamed of Liam, the skinny boy in the Dolly Parton jumper of many colours.

"There was a look of her about you with the blonde hair."

"Was she blonde?" I asked remembering the tall girl from first class, but she had dull blonde hair, not shiny blonde like my wig.

"She was and at the time of the Big Wind…"

"Storm Debbie, you mean?"

"I mean that auld hurricane that blew the slates off the roof of the Home. Well that time of the Big Wind, I was told to bath Brigid and wash her hair because there was an American couple coming to see the children. Poor Brigid's hair was always dull but that day it shone golden just like the wig you're wearing now, Arlene."

"Do I look like her?"

"There's a look of her about you, that's why for a minute I was thinking you was her grown up."

"Grown up?"

"She was only a girleen the time the Americans came but now she'd be as big as yourself, Arlene."

I wanted to keep talking to Delia, but something caught her eye. She stood up abruptly and went over to Maggie. Instead of one slice of Swiss roll, Maggie was holding two slices in her hand and biting into them.

"Maggie, stop stuffing yourself! Do you want to be sick? How many times did I tell you, you can't eat so much sweet cake?"

Maggie shoved the lot into her mouth before Delia could take it from her.

"You'll be up all night with pains in your belly. Come on, we are going home." She caught Maggie by the shoulder and pushed her towards the door. Maggie leaned her hand back and grabbed a fistful of Kerry Cream biscuits from the table.

Maura McLoughlin was coming in as the two women were going out. I forgot I looked like the Home Baby Brigid because I went to speak to Maura and welcome her home.

"Maura, you look great!"

"That's ever so sweet of you to say so."

I hid my surprise at her English accent and just thought she looked beautiful with her raven black hair and big, green eyes.

"Your mother is delighted you're home."

"Yes, Mum was thrilled when I arrived and gave me such a big cuddle."

"Well, enjoy yourself, Maura," I said as I moved away and

joined my friends, wondering if Mrs McLoughlin knew she was giving 'cuddles' now instead of hugs.

Ev kept looking towards the door and I knew why when towards the end of the night Ricky appeared. He had a bottle of whiskey under his jumper which nearly slipped out when he gestured in an exaggerated Jerry Lewis-type mime to follow him into the kitchen, which we gleefully did.

Once the door was closed, he ordered us to supply him with the equipment he needed to perform the miracle of turning one bottle of whiskey into two.

"Get me a jug so I can empty half the bottle of whiskey into it. Now I'll top up the whiskey in the bottle with orangeade." He poured a glass of the orange-whiskey so we could taste it.

"Ricky, this tastes great, more like orange than whiskey," I said and Kait nodded her head in agreement. While we were passing the glass from one to the other, he was filling the half empty bottle of orange with the whiskey from the jug.

"You're a genius, Ricky, now we have two bottles of booze," Ev said plasmásing him.

"Easy, girls. Don't get pissed until we are gone, or we'll get the blame," he said taking Evelyn by the hand.

We sang and danced and acted the eejit and bumped against each other which seemed so funny and made us screech with laughter all the time while drinking our whiskey-drowned orangeade.

The house was emptying in stages. First there were lots of people and then less until only me, Kait and Úna were there. We decided to walk Úna home and took what was left of the Ricky's booze for the journey. Once we were away from Kilmartin

Road, we passed the bottle to each other, sipping from the neck like we had seen Jim and Ricky do.

When we got to the station, we decided we'd go up the tracks for old times' sake. Kait was already tipsy, tripping over the tracks, so me and Úna got on each side of her and linked her arms until we got to the ditch with the gap. We pushed her through it into the old graveyard. She started singing *Raindrops keep falling on my head*, and we joined in as we tumbled from grave to grave. Every now and then one of us would put our finger in front of our lips and say a long 'Sssshhh!' so the dead wouldn't wake and 'appear unto us.' If ever the dead were going to wake, that was the night with our crazy carry on.

In the new cemetery we found a big white marble tombstone and sat on it. We spoke in whispers louder that roars, laughed until our sides hurt and drank until the contents of the bottle got low like Kait's eyelids were getting. She wanted to sleep and lay down next to a glass dome with plastic flowers inside.

Úna said, "My bed is cosier than this cold slab. I'm going home."

She got up and started to walk towards the gate. Her house was on the other side of the road. We trailed behind her to the kitchen door. Her father was inside talking to one of the stupid relations that were always blocking up the kitchen. Naturally, this stopped us from going in, so to get our own back we decided we'd stick our tongues out at the eejit inside and leaned towards the window. I was behind Kait and must have pushed her without meaning to, because she put her hands out to save herself and banged against the windowpane.

The eejit inside leaped up from the chair like a jack-in-the-box and ran towards the cross door. Mr McNulty looked up and saw us. With an angry gesture he ordered Úna to come in which left me and Kait to stumble off. I wrapped my arm around Kait's shoulders, and she put hers around my waist. Somehow or other we got home to our lovely beds.

The Next Day

Getting up for twelve o'clock Mass was a struggle. Mammy knocked on my door a few times. In the end she came in, shook me awake, saying I had to get up for Mass. She went out but left the door open.

My eyes were heavy, difficult to lift up, but she kept calling me from the bottom of the stairs, so I dragged myself out of bed and sleep-walked down to the kitchen.

The tea falling from the spout of the teapot sounded like a heavy downpour and the rattling of the cup on the saucer was louder than thunder. I tried to run from the storm, but Mammy insisted I had a slice of toast which sounded like gravel being dumped on a laneway when she started buttering it. I painfully opened my mouth and forced my teeth to bite off a corner, fooling her into thinking I was eating and allowed me to leave the kitchen. I fell upstairs and into my room. There I fumbled with my clothes and managed to get them on while Mammy's voice from downstairs urged me to hurry or I would be late for Mass.

Outside the door the sun was strong and blinding. I walked up to the chapel with my eyes lowered because the light hurt. When a passer-by saluted me, I couldn't raise my eyelids, I could only squint from under them, not seeing who was greeting me.

Sitting in our usual pew, Kait and Úna were more asleep than awake. Evelyn rushed in at the last minute as lucid and talkative as always. She was as annoying as the old woman rattling her rosary beads in the bench behind me.

After Mass she warned us not to forget to be on the *An Lár* at eight o'clock for The Miami Showband's bus.

Every year the Leaving Cert class hired a bus to go to a dance and celebrate they had finished secondary school. Even though it was their special night – maybe the last time they would ever be together – they didn't mind if girls from other classes went. The bus was expensive to hire, so the more that came and paid their fare, the least the bus cost each girl.

That night of the dance, me, Ev and Úna were giddy on our stiletto heels while's Kait's gait was steadier on her solid block heels. The four of us pushed ourselves in onto a seat meant for three. Coat-pockets bulging with a can of lacquer, comb, stick of pancake make-up and a black eye-liner pencil stopped us for being comfortable, so we took them off. I noticed Ev's lilac Sandie Shaw-type dress was a bit tight around her stomach, but I knew that I was not to say, 'You're getting a bit fat.' Instead, I complimented her on her dress. "Ev, you look gorgeous! Wish my dress was as nice as yours."

"Don't be daft. Even if you were wearing a sack, you'd look a million dollars!"

"I'd give anything to have lovely long, straight hair like yours, Arlene, instead of this awful frizzy stuff," Úna said.

"Úna, your hair looks better than it used to when you were small."

"You look like that Jane Asher who is going out with George Harrison," Kait said, and we believed her because she was living in Liverpool. Kait looked stunning in a blue mini dress.

"Thanks. Ev, I was sure you'd go with Ricky in the car?"

"And miss going with ye? Sure, I'll see Ricky after the dance."

"Is he not coming in?" Kait asked. I knew she was hoping he'd come, and that Jim would be with him.

"No fear of him coming in until he's thrown out of the pub."

"God! A pub! I never want to see drink again," I squealed.

"I didn't like the drink at the beginning either, but Ricky was right when he told me I'd get used to it," Ev explained to us novices.

"So will Ricky be around afterwards to take you home?" Kait asked. Again, she was hoping Jim would be with Ricky, as they were always together.

"He'd better cos Mam and me are off to Dublin on Monday."

"Shopping, is it?"

"No, staying with my uncle for a week."

"A whole week, so a holiday. Lucky you, Ev!" I said thinking of when I went to Cavan for a week.

"No, it's not. Mam thinks I'm a bit pale. Her brother is a doctor, so she'll get him to have a look at me."

Talk shortens a journey, as Nan and Nanny used to say. In what seemed like no time, the bus stopped outside the dance hall, and we were jumping off. However, we were stopped in our tracks from moving forward by the forceful Atlantic winds. Shrieking and laughing, we clung on to each other, battling with the wild wind that tried to hold us back, but we were determined to get to the building. We four tough girls had lived through Debbie and this wind was not going to get the better of us although it did take its revenge out on our hair.

"Your hair is like a banshee's!"

"Look who talking! Yours is standing on end as though you saw a ghost."

We won against the wind and were standing at the door, fiddling with our money, dying to get in and rush to the ladies, which we eventually did and came out in a cloud of lacquer with not a rib of hair out of place, looking like we were ready for Mass and not the craic that followed.

We never sat down, if a boy wasn't begging us to dance, we were on the floor wiggling, shaking and throwing our legs in the air. At one point, Ev stopped dancing abruptly and rushed into the ladies. Surprised, I ran after her. She was kneeling in front of the toilet bowl and trying to vomit. Her stomach was heaving up and down and a few drops of dribble were coming out of her mouth.

"What's wrong, Ev?" I asked as I held back her hair from her face.

"Something I ate that didn't agree with me."

"The drink last night, I'd say."

"That's it alright. I'll never drink again."

She cleaned herself and we went back out to the hall. Rory Callahan was hovering around Kait. When he started to approach her, Ev whispered behind her hand, "I wonder is he wearing salmon coloured underwear?" which made us want to burst out laughing. So as not to let him see us skitting, we headed for the ladies leaving Kait on her own. We heard him say, "Would you like to dance?" which made more laughter surge up. Afterwards, she told us he barely looked at her and didn't speak at all.

Towards the end of the night, our stomachs started to rumble and grumble.

"Let's rush out and get some chips before ye go on the bus," Ev said.

While the band was playing the National Anthem, we grabbed our coats and rushed out to find a chip place singing Joe Dolan's *You're such a good-looking woman*. The wind had tired itself out and was blowing with much less force, so our singing rose above it. The chip place was crowded. We tried to charm our way to the top of the queue, but everyone was as hungry as we were, so we had to wait our turn.

When we got back to the dance hall, with our mouths full of vinegar-soaked chips blown cold by the wind, the bus was gone.

Standing a few feet from the Atlantic Ocean, we thought it would be easier to swim to Boston than walk back to Drumbron. Even walking out as far as the road that lead to our town and thumbing was out of the question because our high heels were not boots meant for walking. Úna took charge as usual.

"Ev, where does that fellow Ricky drink?"

"Plenty of places."

"I know that but tell us the name of one nearby here and go and see if he's there."

"Finn's is just down the road." We followed Ev as she crept in through the side door of Finn's public house. Ricky Martin was at the bar, holding court. He slid off the high stool and came towards us. I felt Kait's intake of breath and knew why when I saw Jim Smith was there too, standing with his arm around Loretta's shoulder.

"Ricky, my friends need a lift home. They missed the bus."

"C'est la vie," Loretta said practicing her French.

Kait stepped back behind me trying to get out of sight, whispering, "C'est la bitch."

I saw Jim's eyes pop and then he quickly took his hand from Loretta.

"Ricky, five can easily fit in your car."

"That may be so, but Jim and I came in Richard's car, and we intended to go back with him," Loretta informed us looking adoringly up at Jim.

"Well, there still room for two more, isn't there, Ricky?" Ev said going towards Ricky.

I pushed Úna forward, "You go home with them, Úna, as you have to get up for work tomorrow."

"And ye?"

"Me and Kait will manage." I wanted Ev to get home as soon as possible because the poor thing had been feeling sick in the toilet.

Kait and I walked outside and watched as they squeezed into the back seat beside Loretta. Kait leaned against me. I felt her body shaking as the car drove off. Her first holiday home ruined because Jim had ignored her completely.

Out of the blue, Rory Callahan appeared in his car on the road outside Finn's pub. He rolled down the window and asked, "Girls, do ye need a lift?" to which I replied that we'd be delighted to get a lift back to Drumbron.

I felt Kait pull herself together and knew she was doing this to appear polite. It would not be fair on Rory to be sulky after him being good enough to give us a lift. On the way back, she went through the motions of laughing and having the craic and kept the flow of conversation going, talking about everything. Rory only spoke to say The Miami was a great showband, one of the best in Ireland.

"They are playing in Sligo next week. I'm going if ye want a lift."

"That's good of you, Rory, but I'm going back to Liverpool tomorrow," Kait told him. His face changed. He forgot to ask me if I wanted to go.

The journey back was much longer than the one going. Rory knew where Kait lived without asking. He brought us straight to her gate. Once we got out of the car and he had driven off, Kait clung onto me and sobbed her heart out.

"Arlene, I love him so much."

"Shush, shush! I know you do."

"He's so handsome."

"I know but if he marries Loretta, he'll have ugly kids as small as leprechauns," I said the wrong thing because she was bawling again.

"Cry your heart out. It will do you good because it will wear you out and you'll fall asleep quick."

"I don't want to fall asleep. I want to think about Jim. He has such beautiful eyes."

"Ok, stay awake. But remember I'll be here tomorrow at twelve. We are going to Wynn's and stuffing ourselves with a big slice of Black Forest Gateau."

"I'm having Chester cake for old times' sake, and I want to go to the bridge first."

"No problem," I said as I hugged her. She shuffled into her garden, her head bent, her body shaking.

I started walking towards Sligo Road and my house.

The next day we sat on the bridge, where we used to see the boys after the Legion meetings and spoke about those long-lost days as if we were old people who had left their youth behind.

"Kait, I thought we were going to make pigs of ourselves? Come on, let's go to Wynn's and do it."

We were on the path walking towards the shop when we were startled by the screaming of tires coming to a halt. Jim Smith jumped out, grabbed Kait by the arm and dragged her towards the car shouting.

"Hey you! Get into the car."

"Why would I?"

"Because you owe me an explanation and an apology."

She pulled away. "I owe you nothing."

"Where were you last night after me getting in my car and going back to Sligo looking for you?"

"How was I to know you were coming back? Do you think I can read minds?"

"You saw me looking at you."

"Glad to know you are not blind. Pity your manners aren't as good as your eyesight." Kait had freed her arm and was turning back to where I was.

"I'm talking to you."

"Talk away, no one's stopping you," Kait said. His face looked so surprised I wanted to laugh.

"Eh, don't be like that, sure I'm only mad because I was dying to see you that night."

She smiled. "We got a lift from Rory Callaghan."

"Rory Callaghan, the shoe boy?"

"He's nice, not ignorant like you."

"Look, I'm sorry for the way I spoke to you."

"You should be," Kait said but she was smiling, her dimples showing.

"Listen, how about meeting tonight?"

"Can't, there's no dances tonight."

"We could meet in Quinn's pub?"

"My mother would have kittens if I went into a pub."

"We could go for a spin."

"If you want to see me, call up to my house."

"I don't know your surname, don't mind where you live."

"You know I'm Kait Kenny and I live in Kilmartin Road."

"Kilmartin Road! You are a bit high and mighty for someone who comes from that place."

"Feic off."

Kait tripped after me. She put her arm through mine and leaned against me, her whole body shaking. I set the tone, strolling slowly until her body was in tune and we headed towards Wynn's, knowing Jim couldn't follow because he had left his car with the door wide open and there were two cars behind it beeping loudly.

"Ar, my heart is singing. The boy I adore drove twenty miles just to see me. He must have left Loretta, jumped into his car and drove the whole way to Sligo just to be with me."

I sang, "*You're a such good-looking woman.*"

"You know, Arlene, I didn't sleep last night because I kept thinking if my father was a bigshot, Jim would be going with me instead of Loretta and blaming Dad because we live in a council house."

This revelation surprised me. I supposed it was because of what I had said about Loretta and Jim's fathers playing golf together, so I tried to flatter Kait. "Jim always liked you. When we were small, he was your knight in shining armour, so you don't have to worry about not being an uptown girl."

She half agreed and started speaking about him and his virtues until Jim was the owner of my ears. Luckily the six o'clock angelus bell stuck and saved me from hearing another word about how handsome and wonderful Jim was.

"Look at the time! I have to go and say goodbye to Delia and to Mrs Lynch."

"I'll go with you to Delia's house."

"So Kait, you are off to Liverpool and the nuns tomorrow?" Delia asked.

"I am, early in the morning."

"What will we do without you? The little fairy girl who has turned into the most beautiful young woman. There mustn't be a boy in Drumbron who's not in love with you."

We laughed thinking of Jim. When we told her we were going to Mrs Lynch's, she said, "I was going to see Kathleen myself, so we might as well go together."

It took Mrs Lynch longer than usual to shuffle along the hall and opened the door. When she saw the three of us her face lit up. "Well, it's either a feast or a famine. Come in or that until I see this fine young lady."

We stayed until very late with Kait talking about Liverpool and the nuns while Mrs Lynch said her daughter Mary Ann was now a nurse's aide in New York. Then we left.

"See you tomorrow, Kait. I'll come at about eight, so we'll have time to talk before the train pulls in."

"I won't be able to sleep thinking of Jim."

"Two nights in a row. Good job you're going back to Liverpool, a grá."

Kait was waiting for me outside my house the next morning bursting with news.

"Arlene, last night after supper and the rosary, Mammy said we'd go to bed. She put the light on in the hall and we were halfway up the stairs when we heard a loud knock on the door. Mammy was sure one of the neighbours had taken a bad turn and wanted her to go for the doctor. When she opened the door, I thought I was dreaming because Jim was standing on the doorstep."

"He actually called up to your house?"

"He did. He asked Mammy if he could speak to me."

"Oh Kait, I'm going to have kittens if you don't tell me what he said."

"He looked into my eyes with his beautiful ones and said, 'If the mountain won't come to Mohammad, Mohammad has to go to the mountain!'"

"Oh, Kait."

"Then he said, 'I'd hug you, but your mother is behind the door with the twig, ready to wallop the head off me if I as much as touch you!'"

"Can you imagine, Jim going to the trouble of finding out where you live and going the whole way to your house," I said.

"Arlene, I wanted to kiss him, but Mammy called me saying, 'Kait, say goodbye to that lad now, *a stóir*, because you have to be up early for England.'"

"I always told you he was crazy about you."

"But why did he leave it until the last day to tell me? Now I won't see him until next summer."

"Yeah, but at least you have all year to think about him."

We had got to the station. Kait got on the train begging me to write and let her know everything about Jim.

Letters

My letters to Kait were full of half truths about Jim, never telling her the stories of Jim being drunk and driving on the wrong side of the road. When the Gardaí pulled him up, he said he thought he was in America. Or the time he swerved the car to avoid hitting a ghost crossing the road.

The judge asked him, "How did you know it was a ghost?"

"She was holding her head in her hands, your Honour."

Jim did his Leaving Cert, which was normal, and passed it, which wasn't normal. Everyone knew his father had paid a boy to sit the exam. The teacher knew too but as Jim's family were 'big people' he pretended not to notice dark-haired Jim had become fair-haired.

On the golf course Mrs Fitzgerald had introduced Jim as Loretta's boyfriend which I forgot to tell Kait, instead I filled pages telling her about Ev coming back from Dublin with a hang-dog look on her face.

"Ev, I never saw you looking so down in the dumps. What's wrong? If you are worrying about the Leaving Cert, sure don't we have the whole year to study."

"It's that my father found out about me and Rick. He's raging mad," Ev said, lowering her eyes and not looking at me which meant she was lying to me.

"Oh my God. How does he know?"

"I'd say someone told him. Mouth?"

"Maybe, so…"

"He's sending me off to boarding school in England."

"Why England?"

"Dad has an aunt a nun in the school, so he wants me where I'll be looked after."

"Why doesn't he send you to your uncle, the doctor, in Dublin?"

"Cos he works a lot."

"But he's married, so his wife will be at home."

"I suppose Dad is afraid Ricky could drive up and see me, so it's England."

This was too much to take in. I stared at her not understanding what I was hearing. How could she leave? Weren't we friends? She had no right to go and leave me on my own.

Anger was rising in me but before I spat out my rage, she hurriedly told me the convent had very strict rules and did not allow any correspondence except with the parents.

While I was trying to deal with this cruel piece of information, she swept briskly towards me, wrapped her arms around my waist, laid her head lightly against my chest and was gone.

I stormed off home and spent the night rehearsing what I would say to her in the morning. That deserter wasn't getting away with leaving me. I needed her with me to do my Leaving Cert. By hook or crook, I would make her stay. There was no way she was leaving me too. Even if I had to stand in front of her father's car to stop her, I would do it.

Early the next morning, while it was still dark and I was sound asleep, Evelyn left Drumbron.

I never got the chance to tell her how much she meant to me. No chance to say that I loved her and how I would miss her, like I missed everyone who had disappeared from my life.

First, Liam vanished, then Nanny Ward, after that it was Nan Gormley. Kait left after the Inter Cert. Michael was forced to go away and now Ev was gone too. I cried out in desperation

"What am I supposed to do on my own without my friends?"

There was no clear answer, only a sketchy sensation that I, too, needed to leave Drumbron.

"How can I do that?

I persisted in asking that part of me that was not interested in answering or clarifying what I had to do. As though to get me off its back, in a flash of insight I knew university was my way out of Drumbron. I grasped it with all my might and decided that after my Leaving Cert, I too would leave the town of my birth.

My heart was broken but my head was in one piece, weaving a thread of thoughts designed to get me out of Drumbron. The web my brain was spinning was beautiful in its simplicity. I just needed to study, obtain good results in my Leaving Cert, go to university and leave like everyone else. I would forge a life outside Drumbron like Michael, Kait and Evelyn were doing.

Glossary of Irish words

Drumbron	The Hill of Sorrow
Cú Chulainn	A strong, handsome warrior of the Knights of the Red Branch of Ulster
A grá mo croí	Love of my heart
Craturs	Creatures
Cratureens	Little creatures. The suffix 'een' means little
Grá on them	Appreciation or a liking for the.
Geansaí	Sweater, jersey. Geansaí is Irish for the Guernsey Island
Tobair Benin	Benin's Well
Bud/buddy	Bod (pronounced 'bud') is the Irish for penis
Dun ná Rí	The King's Vallely
An Lár	The Centre
Boilig	Stomach
Gigeen	Word used by older generation for vagina/little vagina. Gig as in Shelia na Gig
Mar dhea	'As if it were that,' literally. It is used at end of sentence to say it is not true
An bhfuil cead agam dul amach?	May I leave?
An bhfuil said ag caint?	Are ye talking?
Nilimid.	We are not

Words & Expressions

Brothers	The Congregation of Christian Brothers, a teaching order
Eejit	Much softer than idiot, more like calling a person 'harmless'
The Famine	The period between 1845 and 1852, known in Irish as 'An Ar Mór/The Great Killing.' One million Irish died from starvation and another million were forced to flee from Ireland as refugees
Brylcream	A hair cream for men. A hair styling product
Ye/Yous/Yis	The different forms of the plural 'you' that the Irish use
Yerselves	Plural of 'yourselves' that some Irish use

Please Review

Dear Reader, If you enjoyed this book, would you kindly post a short review on Amazon or Goodreads? Your feedback will make all the difference to getting the word out about this book. To leave a review, go to Amazon and type in the book title. When you have found it and go to the book page, please scroll to the bottom of the page to where it says 'Write a Review' and then submit your review. Thank you in advance.

About the Author

Honor Harlow is a woman who thought she was going to live peacefully and quietly in her hometown among the people she knew. Life came along and took her elsewhere. The road she found herself on was bumpy and scary, and sometimes lonely. Against all odds, she kept going, seeing things that changed her. Now she writes what she has witnessed and experienced.

www.ingramcontent.com/pod-product-compliance
Lightning Source LLC
Chambersburg PA
CBHW030254100526
44590CB00012B/400